Ethics, Law and AI

Edited by

Carmine Di Martino (Università degli Studi di Milano)
Federico L.G. Faroldi (Università di Pavia)
Roberto Redaelli (Università degli Studi di Milano)

Volume 1

Roberto Redaelli [Ed.]

Moral Normativity in an Interdisciplinary Perspective

Humans, Animals & Artificial Intelligence

VERLAG KARL ALBER

The Deutsche Nationalbibliothek lists this publication in the Deutsche Nationalbibliografie; detailed bibliographic data are available on the Internet at http://dnb.d-nb.de

ISBN 978-3-495-99428-3 (Print)
978-3-495-99429-0 (ePDF)

British Library Cataloguing-in-Publication Data
A catalogue record for this book is available from the British Library.

ISBN 978-3-495-99428-3 (Print)
978-3-495-99429-0 (ePDF)

Library of Congress Cataloging-in-Publication Data
Redaelli, Roberto
Moral Normativity in an Interdisciplinary Perspective
Humans, Animals & Artificial Intelligence
Roberto Redaelli (Ed.)
141 pp.
Includes bibliographic references.

ISBN 978-3-495-99428-3 (Print)
978-3-495-99429-0 (ePDF)

Online Version
Nomos eLibrary

1st Edition 2023

Table of Contents

Roberto Redaelli

Moral Normativity in Humans, Animals & Artificial Intelligence. An Introduction

Nowadays many disciplines are devoting particular attention from a variety of perspectives to the normative nature of our forms of life. From linguistics to jurisprudence, from anthropology to philosophy, from economics to neuroscience, the subject of moral normativity constitutes a Gordian knot of the present age, towards which the efforts of scientific and philosophical understanding are directed.

The following volume is addressed to achieving a better understanding of moral normativity. It collects works by primatologists, sociologists and philosophers of law, ethicists and phenomenologists, and their contribution to resolving issues regarding the normative profile of ethical concepts, judgments and reasons, i.e., the source of their binding force that guides the behaviour of the human agent.

A primary aspect of this issue, which we address in this volume, is the link between humans and animals, examined in a twofold direction of inquiry. On the one hand, the evolutionary perspective, which questions the natural history of our species, makes a decisive contribution to understanding the origin and nature of human moral normativity. On the other hand, using an ontogenetic perspective, it is possible to recognise forms of proto-normativity in children and animals.

The first two writings that open the volume refer to this framework of reflections. Richard Wrangham's valuable contribution *The transition from might to right: male-male conflict and the evolution of Homo duplex* is aimed at reconstructing the origins of moral normativity starting from an evolutionary explanation. In other words, it is a question of understanding why natural selection favors the extreme form of cooperation that morality represents. The hypothesis advanced by Wrangham is that adult males cooperated in executing tyrants using pre-conceived plans. Those alliances then became social means used to impose group norms that benefited those males. Following this dynamic, Wrangham convincingly shows the emergence of the normative force of moral norms and together with it of the figure of the so-called *Homo duplex*, who is governed by the opposited motivations of selfishness and groupishness.

This first contribution is followed by that of Edoardo Fittipaldi: *Norms, Rights, Obligations: An Attempt at Empirical Reduction*. In this contribution, Fittipaldi conceptualizes norms in terms of psychical dispositions to experience *normative* emotions toward certain behaviors. In turn, *normative* emotions are conceptualized as emotions that emerge during primary socialization by virtue of the manner in which the child conceives of their caregiver, namely, much as monotheisms conceive of the One God. By using this hypothesis (which was first formulated by Bovet, Freud and Piaget), Fittipaldi reconceptualizes the notions of norm, right and obligation, and argues that it makes sense to speak of the existence of proto-norms and proto-rights, as well as of proto- and para-normative emotions, and so both in human and non-human animals.

A second direction of investigation is that developed by the contributions of John Drummond and Alessio Rotundo. These authors address the normative dimension of human being by making use of the phenomenological perspective. The masterful analyses carried out by John Drummond in *The Normativity of Norms* aim to highlight how the normativity of norms is rooted in the structures and goods inherent in the structures of rational experience, where chief among these structures, as Husserl affirmed, is intentionality, the mind's directedness to the world, and chief among these goods is what the author defines as truthfulness. In order to demonstrate this thesis, Drummond's reflections are based on a double distinction, that epistemic and practical norms, and with regard to practical norms, between first- and second-order norms.

Rotundo's contribution aims to highlight and discuss the positions of Maurice Merleau-Ponty and Raymond Aron on interpreting cultural values. Both authors converge around a critique of the relativistic viewpoint advanced by the anthropology of Claude Lévi-Strauss and propose the idea of an ethics predicated on plurality that is not at odds with a reflection on the meaning of rational humanity in history. As clearly shown by Rotundo this ethics assumes in Aron the form of a "pluralist anthropology" and in Merleau-Ponty of a theory of "historical symbolism". The question of moral normativity is thus linked to the ability to hold together the plurality of different cultures without however falling into a form of relativism.

The last two writings that close the volume address the relationship between moral normativity and artificial intelligence. Roberto Redaelli's article *Artificial Intelligence and Quasi-Normativity* aims to investigate the notion of digital normativity, understood as the binding force exerted on the human subject by the predictions and standards established by artificial intelligent systems. In order to explain the AI binding force, Redaelli introduces the notion of quasi-normativity using the post-phenomenological perspective of Don Ihde, who defines AI in terms of quasi-other. With the notion of quasi-normativity the author intends to show how the models generated by AI already possess an injunctive force, linked to the predictive efficiency of algorithms, that redefines to a certain degree our space of freedom and directs our action.

The volume concludes with a contribution by Federico Faroldi who programmatically outlines a solution to the AI alignment problem starting from the Human-Compatible Approach developed by Stuart Russell. This promising approach proposes that intelligent agents be not required to maximize a simple given reward function attached to single aims, but to maximize the realization of human preferences, which are essentially uncertain. By developing this research direction, Faroldi intends to propose methods that will enable AI systems to comply not only with precise rules, but also with ethical principles and moral values. In this sense, the normative issue is addressed starting from a perspective that aims to account for the alignment of artificial intelligence with human values.

By approaching the normative issue from an interdisciplinary perspective, which includes both living beings and non-living things, the book aims to provide the reader with an overview of a series of problems that are increasingly urgent today, and due to which not only the present but also the future of our humanity is at stake.

Richard Wrangham

The transition from might to right: male-male conflict and the evolution of *Homo duplex*[1]

Charles Darwin's 1871 publication of ›*Sexual Selection and the Descent of Man*‹ launched new approaches to normative questions about morality. The concept of a sense of right and wrong had traditionally been explained by reference to divine powers, but evolutionary theory opened the way to investigations of morality using biological and social sciences. The problem was difficult, however. Natural selection was supposed to favor traits that benefit individuals and their kin, not non-kin. Morally right behavior, by contrast, often involves agents sacrificing their own immediate interests for the benefit of a larger group, many or most of whom are not genetically related to the agent. So a critical question became: what could explain the evolution of those moral tendencies underlying unselfish behavior that benefits non-kin? Darwin did not have an answer that satisfied him, and the question has continued to puzzle scholars to the present day.

The problem applies only to humans because although non-human animals can exhibit forms of morality including empathy, prosociality and mutualistic cooperation, only humans have moral tendencies that promote group benefits (de Waal, 2006; Engelmann et al., 2017; McAuliffe and Santos, 2018). Only humans, therefore, conform to Durkheim's (1973) notion of *Homo duplex* – a species in which individuals are torn between their motivations for selfishness on the one hand, and for promoting the interests of their social groups, on the other (Kluver et al., 2014). In the remainder of this essay I use »morality« to refer to the uniquely human forms of moral behavior that are self-sacrificial on behalf of a group or towards individual group members.

---

[1] This paper is an extended and revised version of my text *The Execution Hypothesis for the Evolution of a Morality of Fairness* published in: *Ethics & Politics* (2021) XXIII/2, pp. 261–282.

Several reasons suggest that humans have innate tendencies to behave morally. Emotions are clearly important in moral judgment, given that agents can be committed to moral decisions for which they are unable to produce any rational explanation (i.e. moral dumb-founding, Haidt, 2012). Furthermore in studies of moral decision-making, neural regions have been identified that are more engaged in the production of quick and automatic emotional responses than in slower, consciously reasoned reactions (Greene and Young, 2020). Such emotions are theorized to have an innate component in the form of a norm psychology, i.e. a tendency to acquire norms, comply with norms, and punish norm violators (Chudek and Henrich, 2011; Sripada and Stich, 2006).

Here I present a hypothesis that purports to explain the evolution of a norm psychology and the resulting moral behavior. The proposal, which I call the execution hypothesis, was initiated by Boehm (2008, 2012, 2018) and developed by Wrangham (2019a, 2021). Like many other theoretical investigations of the origins of morality it focuses on cooperation as the critical problem: why did natural selection favor the extreme form of cooperation that morality represents, such that individuals become willing to compromise their own immediate interests for the sake of a larger group?

1. Repression of competition: a critical condition for the evolution of cooperation.

The execution hypothesis can be traced to a theoretical analysis by the biologist Richard Alexander (1987). Alexander argued from first principles that cooperation can evolve among individuals only in the rare condition when a mechanism suppresses competition among them. His argument helped spawn the idea that the repression of competition is a necessary precondition for the evolution of cooperation in general, whether among individual organisms or sub-organismic units (Frank, 2003; Frank, 2013). Such units below the level of the individual include genes (cooperating as genomes) and cells (cooperating as metazoan organisms). The theoretical concept that solves the problem is called the enforcement of cooperation (Ågren et al., 2019; West et al., 2021). A vital question in all such cases is to explain why a mechanism occurs that represses internal competition »in the face of the ubiquitous drive toward individual selfishness« (Frank, 2003, 694).

The most prominent and impactful form of individual selfishness found among the primates to which humans are related is competition for dominance among adult males. In Old World monkeys and apes male-male competition has led to males evolving multiple adaptations for fighting, including large bodies, strong muscles, long canine teeth and high motivation to respond to challenges with aggression. These adaptations have been favored because males who win fights and achieve high dominance status tend to achieve high evolutionary success in the form of elevated levels of paternity and offspring survival. Among humans' primate relatives, this competitive dynamic has invariably led to one male dominating all other males in his social group. The male who vanquishes all others is termed the alpha male. For the alpha male, »might is right.«

Humans, by contrast, do not have alpha males. In small-scale societies of humans there tend to be no leaders, such as among nomadic hunter-gatherers and forest horticulturalists. In larger groups human societies can have leaders, but unlike the arrangement among non-human primates, human so-called leaders do not personally defeat all their subordinates in one-on-one fights. Human leaders achieve their high ranking positions through the support of an alliance. If the leader's allies cease to support him, he will lose his top position.

The fact that hunter-gatherers mostly have no leaders is particularly important given that their societies provide strong indications of the nature of human society in the Late Pleistocene (Boehm, 2012). The lack of alpha males in nomadic hunter-gatherers therefore indicates that by the late Pleistocene, natural selection in humans no longer favored the alpha-male style of behavior. The question is why. What had happened among the males of human ancestors to suppress or modify the »ubiquitous drive toward individual selfishness«?

2. Reduction of competition among males in humans

In an extensive review of small-scale societies Boehm (1999) found occasional cases of individual men using their fighting ability to attempt to dominate other men by threats, bullying or murder. When this happened, Boehm reported, the community would first try to stop the culprit by various forms of persuasion, including verbal confrontation, ridicule and ostracism. If such efforts failed, the community authorised his execution. Boehm (1999) presented evidence that capital punishment is a cultural universal, including being found among hunter-gatherers in all continents.

Boehm (2012, 2018) theorized that over many generations the execution of would-be tyrants would select against aggressive behavior and in favor of prosocial behavior and a sense of right and wrong. This argument is plausible because it invokes two types of aggressive behavior, proactive and reactive aggression, that are elicited by different neural pathways, and therefore can have different evolutionary dynamics (Wrangham, 2018). Executions are planned behaviors that utilize proactive (planned) aggression, not reactive (impulsive) aggression. By contrast the tyrannical behavior that enables a male primate to become an alpha depends on his responding primarily with reactive aggression to challenges from his male rivals. The consistent use of proactive aggression (in the form of execution) to control reactive aggression (as practiced by males competing to be alpha) would have had a predictable evolutionary effect: the propensity for proactive aggression would be maintained at a high level, while the propensity for reactive aggression would be selected against.

Communally approved execution, or capital punishment, is not found in non-human primates (Wrangham, 2021). I have argued that it is restricted to humans because only humans can share their intentions with each other in a sufficiently sophisticated way to confidently kill a physically intimidating tyrant. The difficulties for the killers include not only carrying out the kill but also being sure that the victim's allies will not themselves respond with aggression. An advanced form of language appears to be necessary to negotiate those social complexities (Wrangham, 2021).

3. Self-domestication: evidence for the execution of alpha males in the Pleistocene.

The ability for communally approved execution, once it evolved to the point where it could be carried out safely from the perspective of the »beta-male« killers, is expected to have been used routinely because the killers thereby escaped being dominated by an alpha. The evolution of capital punishment is therefore predicted to have acted against the propensity for reactive aggression (as used by the alpha) and in favor of the kinds of cooperation that would enable suppression of would-be alphas. Remarkably, the expected selection against reactive aggression is evidenced in the fossil record. Shortly before 300,000 years ago, in an immediate ancestor of *Homo sapiens* (often called *Homo heidelbergensis*), skulls start to show a new evolutionary direction that resembles trends found in domestic animals compared to their wild ancestors.

In domesticated animals, experimental selection against reactive aggression leads to the emergence of a »domestication syndrome«, i.e. a characteristic series of anatomical, behavioural, physiological and cognitive traits found at higher frequency in domesticates than in their wild ancestors. Anatomical elements of the domestication syndrome are found in *H. sapiens* compared to *H. heidelbergensis*, including reductions in body mass, brain size and sexual dimorphism, shorter and narrower face, smaller molars and reduced trabecular bone compared to earlier ancestors (Leach, 2003; Cieri et al., 2014; Wrangham 2021). Reductions in two of these traits (face and molars) are first detectable from ~315,000 years ago at Jebel Irhoud in Morocco, a discovery that has led to those fossils being named the earliest known *H. sapiens* (Hublin et al., 2017). Other traits develop *sapiens*-style features at various subsequent times. The initial detection of *sapiens*-style features at ~300,000 years ago thus indicates that by then our ancestors were beginning to lose the alpha-male system.

The idea that many of the anatomical differences between *H. sapiens* and earlier ancestors can be explained as resulting from a domestication-like process has been investigated with genetic data. When compared to their wild ancestors, domesticated species tend to display some genetic changes in parallel, related to features of the domestication syndrome. Although no genetic material is yet available from *H. heidelbergensis*, two species of *Homo* that lived contemporaneously with *H. sapiens* prior to 40,000 years ago offer useful stand-ins for *H. heidelbergensis*: they are *H. neandertalensis* (in Europe and southwest Asia) and *H.* »denisova« (in western Asia). The lineage leading to *H. neandertalensis* and *H.* »denisova« split from *H. sapiens*' ancestors around 500,000 years ago, and neither of those relatives shows the anatomical signs of self-domestication found in *H. sapiens*. Genetic changes associated with mammalian domestication have now been found in *H. sapiens* compared to *H. neandertalensis* and *H.* »denisova« (Theofanopolou et al., 2017; Zanella et al., 2019). In one analysis the time when such genes were initially favoured in *H. sapiens* was narrowed to the expected time, i.e. 500,000 to 300,000 years ago (Andirko et al., 2021). Genomes thus offer *a priori* tests of the hypothesis that *H. sapiens* is a self-domesticated form; and initial tests are supportive.

I therefore assume that the emergence of *H. sapiens* reflects a decline in the propensity for reactive aggression. Accordingly we need to consider why selection no longer favored alpha-style behavior among males. At least eight alternatives to communally approved execution have been suggested, including group-structured culture selection (also known as cultural group selection); social selection by female mate choice; social selection by male partner choice; increased self-control; cooperative breeding; high population density; and use of lethal weapons. Wrangham (2019b) concluded that none of these alternatives is viable. An important problem for most hypotheses is that they do not explain how males would have been constrained from using violence to promote their selfish goals.

In short, the evidence in human evolution of a domestication-like process, which must have been self-domestication rather than domestication by any other species, supports the notion that the transition to *H. sapiens* was associated with a reduction in the propensity for reactive aggression and therefore very likely by the emergence of communally approved execution.

4. Implication of communally approved execution for the evolution of morality.

In independent small-scale societies today, the legitimate use of violence is monopolized by an alliance of male elders who organize or permit executions conducted in defence of social norms. According to the execution hypothesis, essentially the same monopoly on the legitimate use of violence has been maintained throughout the >300,000-year existence of *H. sapiens*, elaborated nowadays by institutions including law and religion. This inference suggests that on the one hand, the ultimate source of ethical concepts such as justice is the set of norms created or approved by such a male alliance; and on the other hand, the ultimate source of individuals' readiness to conform to such concepts is the selective pressure of capital punishment that killed non-conformists throughout the last

300,000 to 400,000 years. According to this analysis, human social-psychological tendencies have thus evolved to be deeply, albeit often subconsciously, self-protective by promoting conformity to group norms. The effectiveness of recent non-lethal forms of punishment such as prisons, castration, fines and exile has reduced the frequency of execution, but Pleistocene principles still hold: non-conformists are punished in ways that stop them from undermining the interests of the male alliance, and the incidental effect is that the genetic fitness of the non-conformists tends to be reduced, leading to selection against antisocial behavior.

Human moral intuitions tend to protect agents from accusations of immorality by pushing agents towards plausibly deniable and/or conforming actions (Wrangham, 2019a). For example the »Action/Omission« bias describes individuals preferring omission to commission. The »Means/Side- Effect« bias pushes agents from actions that intentionally lead to harm. The »Contact/Non-contact« bias reflects efforts to avoid touching someone who is being harmed. A bias for conformity means that moral decisions are strongly influenced by social context (Kundu and Cummins, 2013), even when »social context« is as limited as the presence of two black spots that resemble eyes (Engelmann et al., 2016). The tendency for morally guided actions to be conformist and self-protective fits the proposal that social punishment has been a key component of the evolution of the moral senses, leading to a morality that serves the prevailing ethics of the group, or a power-wielding subgroup, rather than being derived from any rationally derived absolute (Paley, 2021).

5. Intergroup competition: the traditional hypothesis

Moral behaviour is widely agreed to reduce competition and conflict, and therefore to benefit group members on average (Burkart et al., 2018; Curry et al., 2019a). The execution hypothesis proposes that this positive relationship between morality and benefits began as an incidental consequence of the way that group males resolved conflicts among themselves: males first developed a newly sophisticated style of cooperation to kill alphas, and then adapted that skill towards promoting a broader set of their interests. By contrast, a longer tradition sees the benefits of group-level cooperation as being the primary reasons why morality evolved. Various potential benefits of cooperation have been proposed, such as increased food-sharing within groups (Tomasello, 2016) or increased resource sharing between groups (Spikins et al., 2021), but the most frequently proposed candidate is an increased effectiveness in intergroup competition (Choi and Bowles, 2007).

A leading example of a theory explaining morality at least partly as an adaptation for increasing group competitive ability is the ecological dominance social competition model (EDSC) developed by Alexander (1971, 1979, 1982, 1987, 1990) (Flinn et al., 2005; Summers et al., 2020). Alexander suggested that during the Pleistocene, *Homo* groups had overcome the hostile forces of nature sufficiently well that social competition in general, and warfare in particular, became predominant selective forces on their behaviour. Under these conditions selection favoured groups whose members were the most moral, and who therefore became the most cooperative and successful in intergroup competition.

In support of this premise, warfare was likely an important selective pressure in the Pleistocene (Glowacki et al., 2020). Numerous experiments and observations show that intergroup competition tends to increase within-group cooperation in humans (Bauer et al., 2016, Henrich and Muthukrishna, 2021), as well as in other species (chimpanzees: Brooks et al., 2021, Samuni et al., 2020; birds and mammals: Radford et al., 2016). Within-group cooperation can also increase the likelihood of winning intergroup conflicts (Turchin et al., 2013).

In many ways the EDSC and the execution hypothesis are reconcilable. Alexander (1982) proposed that moral systems developed when individuals gained the cognitive ability to manipulate other group members into cooperating, including in ways that would aid their group in intergroup competition. The conferring of rewards and punishments was critical. Systems of indirect reciprocity and monitoring of reputations meant that beneficent acts given by an agent to individual A could lead to the agent receiving return benefits at later times from individuals B, C etc. Within such constraints Alexander viewed individuals as constantly striving to maximise net gain. For example whereas Darwin (1871) conceived of a conscience as a device to inhibit immoral behavior, Alexander (1979) saw it as a mechanism for strategizing how morally an agent should behave in a given situation. In Alexander's view selection favoured individuals who gave the appearance of acting for the greater good, even if the appearance was false. Thus an essential feature of Alexander's argument was that morality evolved in response to a tension between the interests of each individual and their group. These concepts are broadly compatible with the execution hypothesis, as Boehm (2012) emphasized in acknowledging Alexander's contributions.

Against the EDSC, however, it does not address the emergence of the reverse dominance hierarchy, it is silent on the question of specifically when morality emerged, and it has not been related to the paleo-anthropological record, including the question of when warfare supposedly became increasingly important. It also faces specific difficulties.

First, an appealing feature of the EDSC model, as it was first conceived, was that it suggested that a unique feature (human morality) was explicable by a unique evolutionary stimulus (exceptionally intense warfare). Subsequent research on intergroup aggression found, however, that chimpanzees experience similar death rates from intergroup aggression as hunter-gatherers (Wrangham et al., 2006). This suggests that although intergroup aggression was important for Pleistocene *Homo* its selective significance was not exceptional. If warfare led to morality in humans, why did it not do the same in chimpanzees?

Second, mechanisms by which morality could have evolved through its effects on intergroup competition in the Pleistocene have not yet been identified (Dyble, 2021). The essential problem is that the free-riders who do not cooperate (do not self-sacrifice) in war would apparently benefit from the self-sacrificial efforts of their peers. Theories of group-structured cultural evolution readily attribute the growing scale of human cooperation in the last 12,000 years to the effects of warfare in promoting group norms (Henrich and Muthukrishna, 2021), but whether such models are applicable to earlier phases of human evolution has not been demonstrated.

In sum, Alexander's theory and the execution hypothesis share the view that morality evolved from social selection of behaviour, with individuals trying to maximise their gain within societies of intelligent, problem-solving, cooperative and competitive egoists. Alexander would likely have agreed with the execution hypothesis in its explanation for an agent feeling s/he has to perform a given moral act. According to both approaches, the proximate explanation would be that the agent should follow the moral rule unless s/he can be confident of escaping the potential costs of a more selfish act;

and the ultimate explanation is that the agent's moral emotions have evolved under social selection in ways that tend to benefit the agent by conforming.

On the other hand, the hypothesis that cooperation for warfare underlies the evolution of morality is weakened by its being untied to the paleo-anthropological record, its silence on the question of how alpha-style violence was selected against, its error in predicting that intergroup aggression would be uniquely important for humans compared to other species, and its lack of a convincing mechanism. No other group-benefit theories are markedly more successful than Alexander's in identifying the social dynamics by which moral behaviour would have been favoured (Dyble, 2021). There is certainly strong evidence that moral rules tend to promote cooperative behaviour and that very similar moral rules are widespread or universal across societies of all types (Curry et al., 2019a, 2019b). But the fact that morality promotes cooperation, whether in food production, food-sharing, caring, war or other contexts, need not explain why and how it emerged.

6. Sex differences in the origin and dynamics of the moral system

A long tradition in moral philosophy treats the moral system as having emerged from cognitive processes for which sex differences are irrelevant. The question of why moral attitudes often favour males over females might then be answered by the idea that males respond to a system that was originally unbiased by sex, and now exploit it to benefit themselves.

In a somewhat parallel way, evolutionary theorists attempting to explain why humans are an »ultrasocial« (highly cooperative) species routinely do so without addressing sex differences in cooperative tendencies, or the presence of major sex biases in institutions that support cooperation. For instance in a major recent review of the topic Henrich and Muthukrishna (2021) did not mention sex differences, while at the same time stressing that the interplay among cultural institutions, social norms and cooperative psychology represents a vital contribution to making humans more cooperative than other species. Again, therefore, the implication is that patriarchal inclinations are secondary developments from a system of elaborated cooperation that evolved in the species as a whole.

The execution hypothesis, by contrast, proposes that from the outset, the driving force for the evolution of morality was the behaviour of adult males. An alpha male's domineering aggression is directed mainly towards his male rivals, not to females. Subordinate males will therefore normally tend to benefit by engineering the removal of an alpha. In typical mammals, the effect is merely to increase the chance that a subordinate male will become the new alpha whereas in linguistically skilled *Homo*, the effect is much better for the majority of subordinates (i.e. for those who would not have replaced the alpha): it means that the alpha position is abolished, and the subordinates become members of the dominant alliance.

In contrast to the predictable benefits to males, how much females would stand to gain from the removal of an alpha male is questionable. The answer should depend partly on how much aggression the females would have received from the alpha, which is unknown. An alpha male *Homo* would not necessarily have behaved towards females in a domineering manner. For instance, gorillas are a species in which the alpha male is about twice the weight of females and entirely dominant to them. Yet the alpha gorilla's aggression towards females is mostly mild to moderate, and sexual coercion is minimal (Palombit, 2014). By contrast, in groups in which females mate with multiple males the rates of aggression from males towards females can be high (Goodall, 1986). In short, with respect to the amount of aggression that they received from males, female *Homo heidelbergensis* might well not have benefited by the change from a male hierarchy headed by an alpha to one headed by an alliance.

In line with the Pleistocene scenario, two of the main institutions that support moral norms in the ethnographic present are overwhelmingly dominated by males, namely law and religion. In every kind of society from small-scale to state, even if females participate importantly in male-dominated institutions, they rarely or never do so as a majority. Unsurprisingly, therefore, the social systems whose moral nature those institutions forge are consistently patriarchal: male interests tend to be prioritized on such diverse questions as who is allowed to eat the best food, what punishments should be given for violation of sexual norms, who inherits what, or who is allowed to punish who (Rosaldo and Lamphere, 1974; Smuts, 1992, 1995; Hudson et al., 2020).

What explains these patriarchal tendencies of contemporary *H. sapiens*? A theoretical possibility is that the patriarchal nature of institutional morality is an example of evolutionary inertia. In other words, it could be a formerly adaptive system that is now, due to changed circumstance, non-adaptive but maintained because of psychological tendencies that are no longer well matched to current circumstance.

Alternatively if the core rationale for the evolution of morality was to constrain the domineering aggression of selfish males, the same ancient logic might still apply. Male reactive aggression has apparently been continuously selected against for at least 300,000 years, but even now, in every society, male violence is still a problem that has to be managed, and is much more of a social problem than female violence. The males who do the threatening have changed from the middle Pleistocene. They are no longer merely tyrants acting in the style of an alpha *H. heidelbergensis* or great ape; now they can also be members of a threatening coalition. But either way, perpetrators of violence must be confronted and constrained. Even though in many ways females suffer worse from male violence than males do, the individuals who have most to gain from stopping males from being violent are arguably other males, since they, not females, are the competitors for genetic fitness. This suggests that even today, patriarchal aspects of the moral system are driven by male efforts to compete for power with other males of their own group.

7. Morality and groupishness

I have focused above on the evolution of moral behavior that benefits the agent's group at the immediate expense of the agent. Moral behavior is based on a sense of right and wrong, and is implemented through a set of psychological adaptations that leads agents to follow norms and punish norm violators. Since moral behavior tends to promote cooperation (Curry, 2019a, b), the hypothesis that a norm psychology evolved in response to the ability of a self-serving male alliance to execute tyrants provides an explanation for one important mechanism of cooperation. A norm psychology is not the only biologically based motivational system that promotes cooperation in humans, however.

Another is what Durkheim (1995) called collective effervescence (Shilling and Mellor, 1998). Collective effervescence has been characterized as an amplified, excited reaction that happens when a group of people experience something emotional together, leading to »self-categorization as a member of a group, a sense of union with others, positive affect and prosocial behavior« (Páez et al., 2015: 713). Its effects are enhanced by performance of synchronized behavior such as singing, marching and dancing.

Because collective effervescence promotes cooperation in a selfless manner, is found exclusively in humans and is apparently independent of norms, the biological evolution of specifically human prosocial tendencies cannot be attributed solely to a norm psychology. Following Haidt (2012), it is therefore useful to characterize the human tendencies for self-sacrificial cooperative behavior as groupishness, in contrast to selfishness. Groupish behavior involves self-sacrifice on behalf of a group. The self-sacrifice can vary from a relatively minor loss of individual agency (in collective effervescence) to important risk taking (such as when helping others who are in danger).

Groupishness, accordingly, includes a norm psychology and collective effervescence, and possibly other mechanisms as well. An obvious possibility is that norm psychology and collective effervescence evolved in response to the same pressure, that is, to the ability of groups to collectively punish individuals with excessively antisocial or inadequately prosocial tendencies.

8. Conclusion: the transition from Might to Right and the emergence of Homo duplex

In *Civilization and its Discontents,* Sigmund Freud (1989: 49) claimed that »Human life in common is only made possible when a majority comes together which is stronger than any separate individual and which remains united against all separate individuals… The power of this community is then set up as ›right‹ in opposition to the power of the individual, which is condemned as ›brute force‹. This replacement of the power of the individual by the power of the community constitutes the decisive step of civilization.« By suggesting that the concept of ›right‹ emerged out of primitive power dynamics Freud's thinking encapsulated the essential theory of the origin of morality that I have outlined here. Freud's speculation is now well supported, because humans are the only primates in which societies are dominated not by independent tyrants but by coalitions that have ultimate power to constrain physical bullying by a tyrant, even in societies that have a leader.

A crucial question for understanding human communal action, therefore, is why groups dominated by unconstrained tyrants gave way to societies led by communal action. I have reviewed two major kinds of explanation. The intergroup competition hypothesis proposes that intense warfare could have favoured cooperation among adult males at the expense of tyrants. The idea finds little support. The execution hypothesis proposes that linguistic skills could have enabled adult males to cooperate in executing tyrants using pre-conceived plans or understandings. The execution hypothesis is supported by much ethnographic, genetic, fossil and comparative evidence. The origin of *Homo sapiens* is signalled as the time when selection first started acting to reduce the psychological drive to be a selfish tyrant, and started to favour a norm psychology and probably other components of groupishness.

From that time onwards, humans differed from their cousin species by having »an inner life [that] has something that is like a double center of gravity« (Durkheim, 1973: 152). The addition of groupishness to selfishness as a core motivation has resulted in an internal tension not experienced by other organisms. We are *Homo duplex,* Durkheim wrote, condemned to an endless struggle to satisfy the two contrary beings within us. He described this duality of human nature as part egoism, part morality, and noted that these two motivations »mutually contradict and deny each other… there is a true antagonism between them [because] [t]here is no moral act that does not imply a sacrifice« (Durkheim, 1973: 152).

The classic puzzle is how natural selection could have favored behavior that was self-sacrificial. The answer, I have suggested, is that although moral behavior involves a short-term sacrifice, in the long run individuals benefited from their moral (groupish) tendencies by demonstrating their positive value to the group and thereby saving themselves from the risk of severe punishment, ultimately execution. The emergence of an ability to safely kill group members transformed us into both *Homo sapiens* and *Homo duplex.*

Acknowledgments

I thank the late Christopher Boehm and Brian Hare for longterm collaboration, Chet Kamin, Diane Rosenfeld and Bill Zimmerman for discussion, Barb Smuts for comments, and Bernie Crespi, Mark Flinn and Kyle Summers for advice about Richard Alexander's thinking. Thanks to Roberto Redaelli for the invitation to participate in the conference on ›Rethinking the Sources of Normativity in Ethics‹ (Friedrich-Alexander-Universität Erlangen-Nürnberg, March 2021).

References

Ågren, J. A., Davies, N. G., & Foster, K. R. (2019). Enforcement is central to the evolution of cooperation. *Nature, Ecology and Evolution, 3*(7), 1018–1029. https://doi.org/10.1038/s41559-019-0907-1

Alexander, R. D. (1971). The search for an evolutionary philosophy of man. *Proc Roy Soc Victoria, 84*, 99–120.

Alexander, R. D. (1979). *Darwinism and Human Affairs*. University of Washington Press.

Alexander, R. D. (1982). Biology and the moral paradoxes. *J.Social. Biol. Struct., 5*, 389–395.

Alexander, R. D. (1987). *The Biology of Moral Systems*. Aldine de Gruyter.

Alexander, R. D. (1990). *How did humans evolve? Reflections on the uniquely unique species*. The University of Michigan.

Andirkó, A., Moriano, J., Vitriolo, A., Kuhlwilm, M., Testa, G., & Boeckx, C. (2021). Fine-grained temporal mapping of derived high-frequency variants supports the mosaic nature of the evolution of Homo sapiens. *bioRxiv 2021.01.22.427608*. https://doi.org/doi.org/10.1101/2021.01.22.427608

Bauer, M., Blattman, C., Chytilová, J., Henrich, J., Miguel, E., & Mitts, T. (2016). Can war foster cooperation? *Journal of Economic Perspectives, 30*, 249–274. https://doi.org/dx.doi.org/10.1257/jep.30.3.249

Boehm, C. (1999). *Hierarchy in the forest: the evolution of egalitarian behavior*. Harvard University Press.

Boehm, C. (2008). Purposive social selection and the evolution of human altruism. *Cross-Cultural Research, 42*(4), 319–352.

Boehm, C. (2012). *Moral Origins: The Evolution of Virtue, Altruism, and Shame*. Basic Books.

Boehm, C. (2018). Collective intentionality: A basic and early component of moral evolution. *Philosophical Psychology, 31*(5), 680–702. https://doi.org/DOI: 10.1080/09515089.2018.1486607

Brooks, J., Onishi, E., Clark, I. R., Bohn, M., & Yamamoto, S. (2021). Uniting against a common enemy: Perceived outgroup threat elicits ingroup cohesion in chimpanzees. *PLoS ONE, 16*(e0246869), 1–17. https://doi.org/doi.org/10.1371/journal. pone.0246869

Burkart, J. M., Brügger, R. K., & van Schaik, C. P. (2018). Evolutionary origins of morality: insights from non-human primates. *Frontiers in Sociology, 3*(17), 1–12. https://doi.org/10.3389/fsoc.2018.00017

Choi, J.-K., & Bowles, S. (2007). The coevolution of parochial altruism and war. *Science, 318*, 636–640.

Chudek, M., & Henrich, J. (2011). Culture–gene coevolution, norm-psychology and the emergence of human prosociality. *Trends in Cognitive Sciences, 15* (5), 218–226. https://doi.org/10.1016/j.tics.2011.03.003

Cieri, R. L., Churchill, S. E., Franciscus, R. G., Tan, J., & Hare, B. (2014). Craniofacial feminization, social tolerance, and the origins of behavioral modernity. *Current Anthropology, 55*, 419–443. https://doi.org/http://www.jstor.org/stable/10.1086/677209

Curry, O. S., Chesters, M. J., & Van Lissa, C. J. (2019b). Mapping morality with a compass: Testing the theory of ›morality-as-cooperation‹ with a new questionnaire. *Journal of Research in Personality, 78*, 106–124. https://doi.org/https://doi.org/10.1016/j.jrp.2018.10.008

Curry, O. S., Mullins, D. A., & Whitehouse, H. (2019a). Is It Good to Cooperate? Testing the Theory of Morality-as-Cooperation in 60 Societies. *Current Anthropology, 60*(1), 47–69.

de Waal, F. B. M. (2006). *Primates and Philosophers: How Morality Evolved*. Princeton University Press.

Durkheim, É. (1973 (1914)). The dualism of human nature and its social conditions. In R. N. Bellah (Ed.), *Emile Durkheim on Morality and Society: Selected Writings* (pp. 149–163). University of Chicago Press.

Durkheim, É. (1995 (1912)). *The Elementary Forms of Religious Life*. The Free Press.

Dyble, M. (2021). The evolution of altruism through war is highly sensitive to population structure and to civilian and fighter mortality. *Proceedings of the National Academy of Sciences, 118*(e2011142118), 1–6. https://doi.org/10.1073/pnas.2011142118

Engelmann, J. M., Clift, J. B., Herrmann, E., & Tomasello, M. (2017). Social disappointment explains chimpanzees' behaviour in the inequity aversion task. *Proceedings of the Royal Society B, 284*, 20171502. https://doi.org/doi.org/10.1098/rspb.2017.1502

Engelmann, J. M., Herrmann, E., & Tomasello, M. (2016). The effects of being watched on resource acquisition in chimpanzees and human children. *Animal Cognition, 19*(1), 147–151.

Flinn, M. V., Geary, D. C., & Ward, C. V. (2005). Ecological dominance, social competition, and coalitionary arms races: Why humans evolved extraordinary intelligence. *Evolution and Human Behavior, 26*, 10–46. https://doi.org/10.1016/j.evolhumbehav.2004.08.005

Frank, S. A. (2003). Perspective: repression of competition and the evolution of cooperation. *Evolution, 57*(4), 693–705.

Frank, S. A. (2013). A new theory of cooperation. In K. Summers & B. Crespi (Eds.), *Human Social Evolution. The Foundational Works of Richard D. Alexander* (pp. 40–47). Oxford University Press.

Freud, S. (1989 (1930)). *Civilization and Its Discontents* (J. Strachey, Ed.). W. W. Norton.

Glowacki, L., Wilson, M. L., & Wrangham, R. (2020). The evolutionary anthropology of war. *Journal of Economic Behavior and Organization, 178,* 963–982. https://doi.org/10.1016/j.jebo.2017.09.014

Goodall, J. (1986). *The Chimpanzees of Gombe: Patterns of Behavior.* Harvard University Press.

Greene, J. D., & Young, L. (2020). The cognitive neuroscience of moral judgment and decision-making. In M. S. Gazzaniga (Ed.), *The Cognitive Neurosciences* (Vol. 6). MIT Press.

Haidt, J. (2012). *The Righteous Mind: Why Good People Are Divided by Politics and Religion.* Pantheon.

Henrich, J., & Muthukrishna, M. (2021). The origins and psychology of human cooperation. *Annual Review of Psychology, 72,* 207–240. https://doi.org/10.1146/annurev-psych-081920-042106

Hublin, J.-J., Ben-Ncer, A., Bailey, S. E., Freidline, S. E., Neubauer, S., Skinner, M. M., Bergmann, I., Le Cabec, A., Benazzi, S., Harvati, K., & Gunz, P. (2017). New fossils from Jebel Irhoud, Morocco and the pan-African origin of Homo sapiens. *Nature, 546,* 289–292.

Hudson, V. M., Bowen, D. L., & Nielsen, P. L. (2020). *The First Political Order: How Sex Shapes Governance and National Security Worldwide.* Columbia University Press.

Kluver, J., Frazier, R., & Haidt, J. (2014). Behavioral ethics for Homo economicus, Homo heuristicus, and Homo duplex. *Organizational Behavior and Human Decision Processes, 123,* 150–158. https://doi.org/10.1016/j.obhdp.2013.12.004

Kundu, P., & Cummins, D. D. (2013). Morality and conformity: The Asch paradigm applied to moral decisions. *Social Influence, 8*(4), 268–279, DOI: https://doi.org/10.1080/15534510.2012.727767

Leach, H. (2003). Human domestication reconsidered. *Current Anthropology, 44*(3), 349–368. https://doi.org/10.1086/368119

McAuliffe, K., & Santos, L. R. (2018). Do animals have a sense of fairness? In K. Gray & J. Graham (Eds.), *Atlas of Moral Psychology* (pp. 393–400). Guilford Press.

Páez, D., Rimé, B., Basabe, N., & Wlodarczyk, A. (2015). Psychosocial effects of perceived emotional synchrony in collective gatherings. *Journal of Personality and Social Psychology, 108,* 711–729. https://doi.org/10.1037/pspi0000014

Paley, C. (2021). *Beyond Bad: How Obsolete Morals Are Holding Us Back.* Hodder & Stoughton.

Palombit, R. A. (2014). Sexual conflict in nonhuman primates. *Advances in the Study of Behavior*, 46, 191–280.
Radford, A. N., Majolo, B., & Aureli, F. (2016). Within-group behavioural consequences of between-group conflict: a prospective review. *Proc R Soc B, 283*(20161567),1–10. https://doi.org/http://dx.doi.org/10.1098/rspb.2016.1567
Rosaldo, M. Z. (1974). Women, culture and society: a theoretical overview. In M. Z. Rosaldo & L. Lamphere (Eds.), *Woman, Culture and Society* (pp. 17–42). Stanford University Press.
Samuni, L., Mielke, A., Preis, A., Crockford, C., & Wittig, R. M. (2020). Intergroup Competition Enhances Chimpanzee (Pan troglodytes verus) In-group Cohesion. *International Journal of Primatology*, *41*, 342–362. https://doi.org/10.1007/s10764-019-00112-y
Shilling, C., & Mellor, P. A. (1998). Durkheim, morality and modernity: collective effervescence, homo duplex and the sources of moral action. *British Journal of Sociology*, *49*(2), 193–209. https://doi.org/10.2307/591309
Smuts, B. B. (1992). *Male aggression against women: an evolutionary perspective.* Human Nature, 3, 1–44.
Smuts, B. B. (1995). The evolutionary origins of patriarchy. *Human Nature, 6*, 1–32.
Spikins, P., French, J. C., John-Wood, S., & Dytham, C. (2021). Theoretical and methodological approaches to ecological changes, social behaviour and human intergroup tolerance 300,000 to 30,000 BP. *Journal of Archaeological Method and Theory*, *28*(1), 53–75. https://doi.org/10.1007/s10816-020-09503-5
Sripada, C. S., & Stich, S. (2006). A framework for the psychology of norms. In P. Carruthers, S. Laurence, & S. Stich (Eds.), *Evolution and Cognition. The Innate Mind*, Vol. 2. Culture and Cognition (pp. 280–301). Oxford University Press.
Summers, K., Crespi, B. J., & Flinn, M. V. (2020). Were Humans Their Own Most Important Selective Pressure for Cooperation and Morality? A Critical Review of Richard Wrangham's The Goodness Paradox. *Evolutionary Behavioral Sciences*. https://doi.org/10.1037/ebs0000203
Theofanopoulou, C., Gastaldon, S., O'Rourke, T., Samuels, B. D., Martins, P. T., Delogu, F., Alamri, S., & Boeckx, C. (2017). Self-domestication in Homo sapiens: Insights from comparative genomics. *PLoS ONE*, *12*(10), e0185306. https://doi.org/https://doi.org/10.1371/journal.pone.0185306
Tomasello, M. (2016). *A Natural History of Human Morality*. Harvard University Press.
Turchin, P., Currie, T. E., Turner, E. A. L., & Gavrilets, S. (2013). War, space, and the evolution of Old World complex societies. *Proceedings of the National Academy of Sciences*, *110*(41), 16384–16389. https://doi.org/10.1073/pnas.1308825110
West, S. A., Cooper, G. A., Ghoul, M. B., & Griffin, A. S. (2021). Ten recent insights for our understanding of cooperation. *Nature, Ecology and Evolution*, *5*(4), 419–430. https://doi.org/10.1038/s41559-020-01384-x

Wrangham, R. W. (2018). Two types of aggression in human evolution. *Proceedings of the National Academy of Sciences, 115*(2), 245–253. https://doi.org/10.1073/pnas.1713611115

Wrangham, R. W. (2019a). *The Goodness Paradox: The Strange Relationship Between Virtue and Violence in Human Evolution*. Alfred A. Knopf.

Wrangham, R. (2019b). Hypotheses for the evolution of reduced reactive aggression in the context of human self-domestication. *Frontiers in Psychology, 10*(1914), 1–11. https://doi.org/10.3389/fpsyg.2019.01914

Wrangham, R. W. (2021). Targeted conspiratorial killing, human self-domestication and the evolution of groupishness. *Evolutionary Human Sciences, 3*(e26), 1–21. https://doi.org/10.1017/ehs.2021.20

Zanella, M., Vitriolo, A., Andirko, A., Martins, P. T., Sturm, S., O'Rourke, T., Laugsch, M., Malerba, N., Skaros, A., Trattaro, S., Germain, P.-L., Mihailovic, M., Merla, G., Rada-Iglesias, A., Boeckx, C., & Testa, G. (2019). Dosage analysis of the 7q11.23 Williams region 1 identifies BAZ1B as a major human gene patterning the modern human face and underlying self-domestication. *Science Advances, 5*(eaaw7908). https://doi.org/10.1126/sciadv.aaw7908

Edoardo Fittipaldi[1]

Norms, Rights, Obligations: An Attempt at Empirical Reduction

1. Introduction

The theoretical entity called »norm« is used very often by social scientists to explain or predict human behavior[2]. For example, the fact that John reciprocates a favor he received from Mary can be explained

- either economically, by hypothesizing that John fears that Mary might not do him new favors in the future should he not reciprocate
- or normatively, by hypothesizing that John complies with the *norm* that favors should be reciprocated; a norm he adheres to no matter whether he will ever meet again Mary in the future.

The distinction between economic and normative behavior is crucial to social sciences, however, as was stated in 1968 by Jack Gibbs »despite the plethora of normative explanations, the conceptual treatment of norms remains unsatisfactory« (212). The situation has hardly changed today.

In this chapter I propose a stipulative conceptualization for »norm«, as well as for such modal verbs as »should« and »can« and such nouns as »right« and »obligation«. This conceptualization aims at tracing the referents of these terms to the domain of empirical phenomena without doing away with the distinction between economic and normative behavior; where by *normative behavior* I provisionally understand *a behavior that is taken*

---

[1] I wish to thank Paolo Di Lucia, Riccardo Mazzola, Ignasi Terradas Saborit, and Sergei Talanker (in alphabetical order)—who read a previous version of this chapter—for their invaluable comments and critiques. All errors are my own. This article elaborates on some ideas presented in Fittipaldi 2021a.

[2] Throughout, I use behavior as hypernym for action and abstention.

by a social actor because they believe that it is conformable to a norm (1) *to which they adhere and* (2) *of which they regard themselves as an addressee.*

What I expound here is a *stipulative* conceptualization. I do not believe that there must necessarily be one single stipulative conceptualization for »norm« (or any other term). Due to space limitation, here I do not discuss alternative proposals. Such proposals may be perfectly suitable for scientific goals other than mine, or else draw boundaries between economic and normative behavior other than those drawn here, and I cannot rule out that such different boundaries may turn out to be as scientifically legitimate[3] as the one proposed here—or even more so.

To avoid misunderstandings, though, it should be pointed out that my conceptualization of *normative* phenomena[4] differs in a crucial respect from other conceptualizations: here altruism, benevolence, love, sympathetic concern for others and the well-being of society are *not* conceptualized as *normative* phenomena. This does not mean that I deny the importance of these phenomena among animals (including human animals). However, the phenomena I select here do not intersect with altruistic phenomena[5] and only in some cases do they intersect with prosocial ones.[6]

---

[3] By »scientific legitimacy« of a concept I understand its ability to select causal antecedents in causal laws or to select clusters phenomena whose co-occurrence is over-average (e.g., the symptoms of many psychiatric disorders). This notion elaborates on Petrażycki's notion of *wissenschaftliche Legitimation* of a concept (see, e.g., Petrażycki 1908/1933, 97).

[4] Most scholars refer to what I deal with here as *moral* phenomena.

[5] As will be explained below, this holds also for behaviors taken by a social actor to avert their own anticipated guilt for not behaving that way.

[6] My approach is indebted with those of Leon Petrażycki and Axel Hägerström. For a discussion, see Fittipaldi 2016a. It is also influenced by the notions for »norm« provided by Theodor Geiger and Niklas Luhmann, whose shortcomings my proposal attempts to overcome. For a discussion of those shortcomings, see Fittipaldi 2021a. A notion of »norm« completely different from the one proposed here can be extracted from Haidt's notion of »moral emotion« (where Haidt uses »moral« in the sense I use »normative«). Haidt identifies two prototypical features of »morality«, or—to be precise—of a *moral* emotion: (1) its having disinterested elicitors and (2) its prosociality. It follows that the overall *degree* of morality of an emotion increases along with both its degree of disinterestedness and its degree of prosociality. Two consequences of this conceptualization are that (i) the sense of right, or entitlement, when experienced to protect one's own interest rather than somebody else's one, should not be regarded as a moral emotion and that (ii) it seems not to conceptualize as a *moral* phenomenon

The sole criteria according to which the conceptualization proposed here should be evaluated are:

1. Its logical consistency;
2. Its empirical nature;
3. Its scientific legitimacy, that is, its ability to select antecedents in at least one causal law or to select a cluster of phenomena with an over-average probability of co-occurrence.[7]

This chapter is organized as follows. In Section 2, I propose my conceptualization for »norm«; a conceptualization based on a psychoanalytically-influenced hypothesis concerning the way normative emotions emerge during childhood and perpetuate themselves into adolescence and adulthood, and where I also clarify why this approach does not involve any circularity. In Section 3 and its subsections, I discuss some types of norm, right, and obligation that the different normative emotions give rise to. For each normative emotion I also briefly discuss whether (1) that same emotion, (2) a forerunner of it— i.e., a corresponding *proto*-normative emotion—, or (3) an emotion analogous to it— i.e., a corresponding *para*-normative emotion—can be possibly found among some non-human animals. In the conclusion (Section 4), I summarize some of the implications of this conceptualization and recap it by means of two tables.

the fact that »[t]he human moral sense … furnishes [people] with motives for acts of violence that bring them no tangible benefit« and thus »the net contribution of the human moral sense to human well-being may well be negative« (Pinker 2011, 622). As I said in text, I do not believe that my conceptualization is the only scientifically legitimate one. My impression is that Haidt's conceptualization captures phenomena of the utmost importance. These phenomena, though, present only *limited overlaps* with those my conceptualization aims at selecting. At any rate, a problem with Haidt's definition appears to be his concept of *prosociality*. It is not clear whether by this term he understands some form of groupishness, the future well-being of a given group$_x$, the past positive effects of a certain type of behavior for the survival of group$_x$ (even if those behaviors are no longer useful), or something else.

7 In the case of the proposal I make here, the causal law may be that norms raise the probability that social actors act against their interest (which does not necessarily amounts to acting altruistically).

2. A conceptualization for »norm« and »normative behavior«, and its theorical premises

By »norm« I understand *a cognitive-emotional disposition that amounts to the tendency to experience one or more normative emotions when having the perception or mental representation of a certain behavior or type of behavior.*

By »normative emotion« I non-exhaustively understand such emotions as anger, indignation, disgust, guilt, shame, guilt, pride.

Based on this definition, examples of norms are:

- Mary's disposition to become angry should she not find the table she reserved at the restaurant;
- John's disposition to experience guilt should he not help a friend in financial need;
- Anna's disposition to experience pride should she succeed in resignedly enduring a very painful disease as a manner to be closer to Jesus' suffering on the cross.

By means of this concept, we can explain and predict certain kinds of behavior which we usually do not characterize as economic. Here are three examples.

First, Mary, upon realizing that there is no reserved table for her, might insist that the owner of the restaurant offer her a discount for the next time she will come there—a behavior she would probably not take should she not have the tendency to become angry under such a circumstance. (*It should be remarked that this behavior may even take Mary a lot of time and prevent her from spending a pleasant evening in another restaurant.*)

Second, John's disposition may prompt him to help financially his friend Greg (who fell into financial need) *to the goal of* not experiencing the unpleasant emotion of guilt.[8]

Third, Anna's disposition may prompt her to show an exceptional self-control in the face of the suffering caused by her disease and even cause her to abstain from taking analgesics.

---

[8] Incidentally, this example shows that Max Weber's concept of *instrumental rationality* (*Zweckrationalität*, where »Zweck« means »goal«) cannot be used to distinguish between economic and normative behavior. This is all the more apparent if John starts saving money *to the goal* of helping Greg, and thus not experiencing guilt.

In some sense, normative emotions work as internal *sanctions*, in each of the three possible uses of this term in English:

1. »Sanction« in the sense of »approval« (Mary's anger, as it were, encourages her to ask for a discount);
2. »Sanction« in the sense of »negative sanction« (John's guilt is, as it were, a punishment for his not helping Greg);
3. »Sanction« in the sense of »positive sanction« (Anna's pride is, as it were, an internal reward for her self-control and—possibly—abstention from taking analgesics).

It goes without saying that defining *norms* in terms of *norm*ative emotions involves a circularity that can be avoided only by providing a *non-normative definition of normative* emotion (and in actual fact what I will do here will be to define normative emotions in terms of superegoic emotions).

In this connection, it should be remarked that a major problem that bedevils the definitions of »norm« provided by psychologists, social scientists, and empirically oriented philosophers is that they define norms by using no less obscure terms like »ought«, »must«, »obligation«, and/or »can«. I confine myself to one example. Enrico Pattaro defines norms as

> Belief[s] ... that ... certain types of action *must* be performed ... anytime a relevant type of circumstance gets validly instantiated. This must unconditionally be so, regardless of any good or bad consequences that may stem from the performance in question.[9] (Pattaro 2005, 97, emphasis added)

It should be also considered that some authors regard the presence of *normative language* as an indicator of the presence of a *normative*

[9] I could offer plenty of further examples, but I prefer to confine myself to this one because Pattaro—unlike the overwhelming majority of authors—, by conjecturing that norms may have a relation with obsessive-compulsive disorders (383), shows that he is perfectly aware that defining norms in terms of »must« is unsatisfactory. Further, since my approach connects many normative phenomena to anxiety phenomena and it is believed that there exists a close relationship between anxiety disorders and obsessive-compulsive ones (DSM-5, 235), my proposal can be regarded as an elaboration on Pattaro's conjecture. In this connection the names of three authors who proposed definitions that do not have the flaw of defining norms in terms of »ought to«, »must«, »can« should be made: Leon Petrażycki, Theodor Geiger, and Niklas Luhmann. However, these definitions confront us with other problems which I have discussed elsewhere (Fittipaldi 2021a; 2022a).

phenomenon, and so without realizing that in doing so they beg the question of how *normative* language can be identified. As is well known, in many languages terms that usually have a »normative« meaning can be used in a »non-normative« way (»He must he arrived by now«) and sentences that do not contain a single »normative« term can be used in a »normative« way (e.g., »We don't do that here«[10]; cf. Tomasello 2019, 122). It seems to me that the only way to solve the problem of distinguishing between normative and non-normative sentences without having recourse to our linguistic intuitions is to provide a non-normative criterion. The criterion proposed here will be the presence of *normative emotions* when certain words or sentences are uttered, provided that these emotions are defined in a non-normative way.

The definition of normative emotions proposed here is as follows. By »normative emotion« I refer to those emotions that

- emerge or get reshaped through the interactions of the child with her caregiver
- provided that they emerge or get reshaped by virtue of certain *unrealistic* features she ascribes to him.[11]

In this way, all circularity is avoided.

Prior to discussing some of the most important normative emotions, it is necessary to clarify what I hypothesize these *unrealistic features* are and how I hypothesize they work within children's psyches, and subsequently within adolescents' and adults' ones.

Basically, this chapter is premised on three hypotheses and one stipulative definition:

1. As long as their helplessness lasts, children experience *respect* toward their caregivers. Following Bovet (1917; 1925/1928, 46) and Piaget (1932/1948, 321), I understand respect as a *blend of love and fear*—a fear that includes first and foremost the dread of losing their caregiver's love and being abandoned by him.

---

[10] It could, perhaps, be objected that the normative meaning, in this second example, gets *abducted*—in a Peircean sense—owing to »here« being placed at the end of the sentence. However, there exist languages (e.g., Italian), where the normative nature of corresponding sentences can be abducted exclusively through suprasegmental phenomena; and such suprasegmental phenomena can be hypothesized to boil down to the expression of such emotions as anger, indignation, or disgust (see below).

[11] Throughout, I refer to the child as she and the caregiver as he.

2. The way children conceive of their caregivers closely resembles the way monotheisms conceive of the One God (Piaget 1932/1948, 380), that is, as an omnipotent, omniscient, omnipresent, and eternal being.[12]
3. Some of the features children use to ascribe to their caregivers keep characterizing the emotions that they learn to experience or get reshaped by virtue of (1) and (2)—and these emotions only.
4. It is these emotions that I refer to as *normative.*

I refer to the emergence or reshaping of emotions based on these three phenomena as *normative socialization,* as distinct from the socialization consisting, say, of teaching facts about the world we live in.

This said, I can now discuss some normative emotions and formulate a few hypotheses about how they emerge or get reshaped (each one in its own way), how different concepts of norms should be adopted depending on the normative emotions that constitute them, and whether forms of normativity can be traced among non-human animals.

3. On some types of normative emotion and the norms, rights, and obligations that they give rise to

In Section 3.1, I discuss anger, indignation, and disgust,[13] whereas Section 3.2 is devoted to guilt, shame, and pride. The reason why the discussion is organized in this way will become apparent during the discussion itself.

---

12 Freud made a similar hypothesis in (1932/1981), where he maintained that adults »exhal[t] the image [of their father] into a deity« (163). Sometimes, I employ the expression "›godlike‹ caregiver« to refer to how children conceive of their caregivers. However, it would be more accurate to say that it is the monotheistic God that is caregiver-like, rather than the other way around. It can be hypothesized that the very idea of a monotheistic God (as a further development relative to the monolatric one) is inspired to the way children conceive of their parents. For this reason, »godlike« will always be written in quotes.

13 Due to space limitations, I cannot discuss contempt. See Fittipaldi 2022a (in Italian).

3.1. Anger, indignation, and disgust

3.1.1. Two types of aggression and their socialization

This Section (along with the next two subsections: 3.1.1.1 and 3.1.1.2) is devoted to the normative emotions that can be reconstructed as forms as forms of *socialized aggression*. Animals, including human animals, are known to have two different forms of aggression: *reactive* and *proactive* aggression. My hypothesis is that among human animals both forms of aggression undergo (normative) socialization, that is, they get reshaped by virtue of the three phenomena mentioned above, in Section 2. The result are two emotions: *anger* and *indignation,* that are here conceptualized, respectively, as forms of *socialized reactive aggression* and *socialized proactive aggression*. They will be discussed in the next two sections. However, prior to doing that, it is in order to clarify how I understand the distinction between *reactive* and *proactive* aggression. My reconstruction is based on the way Richard Wrangham conceptualizes them, with one important modification, though.

Wrangham understands *reactive aggression* as »a response to a *threat* or *frustrating event,* with the goal being only to remove the provoking stimulus« (2017/2018, 2, emphases added). As for *proactive aggression,* he understands it as »a purposeful planned attack with an external or internal reward as a goal, [that] is characterized by attention to a consistent target, and often by a lack of emotional arousal« (Ibid.). It is noteworthy that as examples of proactive aggression he offers not only premeditated homicide and ritual sacrifice but also lynching, bullying, stalking, hazing, torture (Ibid. and 2019, 246), that is, forms of aggression often performed *for their own sake*.[14]

This is why, on the one hand, I adopt Wrangham's conceptualization of reactive aggression, while, on the other, due to the wide variety

[14] This is why I believe the term »instrumental« as a synonym of »proactive« is inappropriate in this context. I am not ruling out that proactive aggression may have evolved as an instrumental emotion that, for example, causes predatory or expansionist behaviors necessary for the survival of the individual or the flourishing of their group. However, among human animals it cannot be (any longer) regarded as a merely instrumental form of aggression. At least once, Wrangham expressly hints at *sadism* (cf. 2019, 29). Here the internal reward appears to be the pleasure of inflicting suffering for its own sake—that is, without any further goal. Therefore, it would not make sense to use the adjective »instrumental«.

of forms of aggression that can be regarded as proactive (especially among human animals), I propose to simplify the concept of proactive aggression and understand it as any form of aggression *other than* reactive aggression. In other words, I understand proactive aggression as any form of aggression *not* performed as a response to a threat or frustrating event—a form of aggression the reward for which may even be nothing but the »fun« of inflicting suffering on a sentient being.[15]

One of the first and main things a caregiver usually teaches his child is to restrain her otherwise unrestrained aggressiveness, whether active or proactive. As I said (Section 3), my hypothesis is that this form of socialization get effected by virtue of the »godlike« manner the child conceives of her caregiver.

Due to her caregiver's explicit and implicit teachings,[16] usually the child learns that it is *safe* to be reactively or proactively aggressive.

i. only in certain ways (e.g., verbally, but not physically) and
ii. only if certain circumstances obtain.

In this chapter, I focus on (ii).

As a consequence of her interactions with her »godlike« caregiver, a child may learn that he tolerates or even encourages her reactive and proactive aggression:

ii.i. *only* against *certain* threats or frustrations[17] and
ii.ii. *only* against *certain* cognitively salient people and/or behaviors.

This process of normative socialization results in children's and subsequently adolescents' and adults' learning to react to some frustrations or cognitively salient people and behaviors:

---

15 A further difference between Wrangham and me might be that I regard not only *reactive* but also *proactive* aggression as an *emotion*. As for »emotion«, I use it broadly to refer any non-cognitive state of consciousness (including physical pain).

16 Among other things, implicit teachings include, not only forms of non-verbal communication, but also judgmental conversations between the caregiver and other people (or between the caregivers) concerning others' behaviors, as well as the mere fact that the caregiver acts in a certain way and the child experiences him as a model.

17 Following Wrangham 2017–2018 (2), I do not distinguish here between threat- and frustration-related aggression.

1. either by *restraining* their aggressiveness;
2. or by non experiencing any fit of aggression at all;
3. or by having completely different emotions, like despair.[18]

In this chapter, though, what is most relevant for us is *not* the fact that children can be socialized into (1) restraining, (2) not experiencing, or (3) even experiencing emotions completely different from reactive and proactive fits of aggression. Rather, *what matters is that at the end of this process two types of aggression get selected*, or, so speak, »survive«. They are:

α. a form of socialized frustration-*related* aggression, or *socialized reactive aggression* and
β. a form of socialized frustration-*unrelated* aggression, or *socialized proactive aggression*.

Stipulatively, from now onwards I will refer to the former as *anger* and to the latter as *indignation*[19].

Based on this distinction, while indignation is a gratuitous form of aggression, anger is not: it is always related to an experience of frustration.

We can now discuss anger and indignation separately.

3.1.1.1. Anger

Anger emerges when the child learns that her caregiver tolerates or even encourages her reactive aggression in the event of *certain* frustrations or threats to *certain* objects that are *important to her*—first and foremost her body.

---

[18] Unfortunately, the reaction of males left by their partners remains all too often one of reactive aggression or a combination of reactive and proactive aggression rather than despair. This notwithstanding, we can hope that the tabooization of violence (including the violence of males against their partners) along with, perhaps, the ongoing biological selection against reactive aggression in contemporary societies, will gradually reduce males' reactive aggression in the event they are left by their partner. (On the selection against reactive aggression, see Wrangham 2019.)

[19] Etymologically, »indignation« refers to the reactive aggression of a person whose honor (*dignitas*) has been harmed. This explains why in Latin *indignari* is a deponent verb (i.e., it is used only in the middle-passive diathesis): »I have been stripped of my honor, therefore I become angry«. Its etymology notwithstanding, I chose »indignation« rather than »anger« because it seems to me that »indignation« is often used to refer to what I mean by »socialized proactive aggression«.

Although the types of threat or frustration that may elicit anger vary dramatically across cultures, most socialized children learn *not* to repress aggression in the event of:

- threats to *their* bodily parts;
- threats to certain objects that are important *to them*, such as *their* clothes or *their* toys; and
- frustrations to such expectations as that to receive *one's* equal or, more generally, »fair« share in resources acquired in a joint effort (I cannot address the issue of how »fair« should be understood).[20]

It should be reiterated that anger, unlike indignation, is *not* gratuitous. This is to say that anger is always elicited when some form of *ownness* is involved, like in the event of:

- threat to an object one experiences as *their own* (e.g., one's hand, one's toy, one's brother) or
- frustration of the expectation of receiving an object one already experiences as *their own* (e.g., one's reserved table at a restaurant, the money owed by one's creditor, one's bathtub fixed by a plumber).

A form of connection to an object one already experiences as *their own* can be traced even in the case of Alter's *mere* expectation of receiving a favor from Ego, where by »mere« I mean in the absence of any (1) consideration or (2) expectation of reciprocation of some favor previously made by him (Alter) to her (Ego).[21] Alter may perfectly experience the object of that promised favor as already his own and therefore experience Ego's failure to keep her promise as a full-blown frustration. This may occur even if he did not in any way rely on Ego's promise and thus her failure did not cause him any damage.[22] [23]

The notion of an *anger-backed expectation* can now be introduced.

---

20 With this example, I am not ruling out that the proneness to this reaction may be genetically encoded (cf. Tomasello 2019, 236). However, it is crucial to consider that, even if genetically encoded, this proneness may be inhibited through socialization, as often occurs in the socialization of cadets in cultures characterized by primogeniture or where slavery or serfdom is present—especially if slaves or serfs are not treated in an overly harsh way.

21 Throughout, I refer to Ego as she and to Alter and Tertius (if present) as he.

22 By »promise« I understand Ego's communication to Alter that she will do something he wishes *along with her implication that she is prepared (or »resigned«—see*

Over time, the children whose frustration-related aggressiveness has been socialized by virtue of their interactions with their »god-like« caregivers *may—if do not necessarily—*:

1. *typify* what they can safely be reactively aggressive against, possibly conceptualize them as *wrongs*, and subsequently
2. *shift their cognitive focus* from the types of event that make them safely angry to the related (»opposite«) events that would not elicit *that* anger and consequently *expect their non-instantiation.*[24]

Typification leads to the conceptualization of *wrongs*, whereas *focus shift* (which presupposes typification) leads to *anger-backed expectations*. Thus:

α. an anger-eliciting type of *action* (e.g., being physically assaulted) may give rise to an *anger-backed expectation* concerning an *abstention* (the expectation of *not* being physically assaulted), and
β. an anger-eliciting type of *abstention* (e.g., one's *not* keeping a promise) may give rise to an *anger-backed expectation* concerning an *action* (the expectation that promises be kept).

Anger-backed expectations play a crucial role in everyday life. To make just one example among many possible ones, if a *healthily* socialized individual does not find the table they reserved at a restaurant, they will become angry and insist that the owner find one for them or at least promise a discount for the next time they will go there.[25]

---

below) to endure his anger should she not act accordingly. More on this naturalization of promising can be found in Fittipaldi 2021b.

23 From these examples it should be clear that I hypothesize that the notions of threat and frustration are inextricably connected to the experience of ownness (myness, yourness, etc.). On the relation between ownness and ownership, see Fittipaldi 2021a. It should also be considered that if Tertius becomes angry because Ego harmed Alter, this happens because Tertius sympathizes with Alter and, as it were, experiences that harm as *his own* harm.

24 To keep the discussion simple, I am discussing this process as though it were of a purely ontogenetic nature. However, it should be borne in mind that both typification and focus shift may require cultural processes that take numerous generations.

25 The issue of healthy and unhealthy anger is closely connected with the topic psychoanalysts refer to as *healthy sense of entitlement vs. under-/overentitlement* (see Fittipaldi 2023, 156). A person with a form of underentitlement is a person who has an excessively *low* proneness to anger. For example, such a person could react to their

If we understand »jural« as the adjective of »right« (and use »legal« as the adjective of »law«), this proposed reconstruction implies that anger-backed expectations can also be referred to as *jural* expectations, and that the notions of *sense of right,* or *entitlement* (as well as *injustice*), must be always traced or related to anger, here understood as a *jural emotion*. To experience a sense of entitlement to some object or behavior amounts to having the disposition to become angry should that object not be given or that behavior not be taken—a behavior that the experiencer construes as belonging to them.[26] This is the way I hypothesize that sense of entitlement emerges.

Anger is not the sole jural emotion, though; even if I will sometimes refer to it as the *primary* one. Different jural emotions may exist within actors other than the experiencer of primary anger (here referred to as Alter), namely, the actor of whom Alter expects a behavior (Ego) and a possible bystander (Tertius). Since Tertius's jural emotion is more easily described than Alter's, I first discuss the former's and then the latter's.

Tertius's jural emotion amounts to his *sympathizing*[27] with Alter and experiencing a form of *vicarious anger* due to Ego's behavior with regard to Alter—an anger that in no way requires that Alter also experiences a corresponding form of primary anger or is at all aware of Ego's one.[28]

As for Ego's jural emotion, it could be referred to as his »acknowledgement« of Alter's *right*. The notion of *right,* though, will be examined below as there is no need to discuss it now to clarify the notion of »acknowledgment«.

---

not finding their reserved table at a certain restaurant by wondering whether they did anything wrong that last time they went there or the like. On the other hand, a person with a form of overentitlement might claim a table at a fully reserved restaurant by arguing that they are a regular high-spending customer.

26 In other words, if Alter has an anger-backed expectation concerning Ego's behavior, Alter, as it were, experiences himself as the owner of her behavior or its result.

27 As for my usage of »sympathy« and »empathy« (as well as related terms), see below n. 51.

28 To be precise, what elicits this jural emotion (as well as all normative emotions concerning others' behaviors) is not the way Ego actually behaves, but the way Tertius *believes* she behaves—even if for a short while. For example, Tertius may perfectly experience a form of vicarious anger because of what a fictional character does to another fictional character (provided the fourth wall does not get broken). This point was first made by Leon Petrażycki (1909–10, 65).

By »acknowledgment of a jural expectation«—which can be referred to as *jural resignation*—I understand Ego's disposition to endure Alter's anger, should she (Ego) not meet what she believes is Alter's jural expectation. In other words, I propose to reconstruct this phenomenon as a form of *resignation* to somebody's anger. Resignation may even involve the readiness to uncomplainingly endure Alter's *physical* violence.[29] Jural resignation should be regarded as a jural emotion in its own right; an emotion that, among other things, may give rise to the ascription to Alter of such rights as a *ius puniendi* or a form of authority.[30]

It is of paramount importance to stress that jural resignation has nothing in common with guilt, which is here understood as a non-jural (or moral) emotion, that is, as a normative emotion that, unlike jural emotions, does *not* involve an Alter who somewhat *owns* something or some behavior (including his own behavior, as in the case of certain easements, like a right of way, or constitutional »rights«, like freedom of speech).

I will discuss guilt below, in Section 3.2.1. However, to avoid misunderstandings it is in order to stress here that guilt and jural resignation may be contemporarily present in Ego for what she believes she did to Alter. My point is that they are different phenomena and, notably, that Ego's *guilt* for not having behaved in some way to the advantage of Alter does not necessarily imply Ego's readiness to endure Alter's anger.[31] For example, Ego may feel guilty for not helping her friend Dneirf, whom she knows is in financial need. But Dneirf's anger at Ego's not helping him (i.e., his experiencing himself as entitled to be helped by her), would probably shock Ego and even terminate their friendship. To use a terminology that I will clarify below, we can say that, if Ego feels guilty for not helping Dneirf but would be shocked by his anger at his not being helped by her, Ego experiences her obligation to help him as a *moral* and not as a *jural* obligation.

---

29 I conjecture that the tendency to raise one or both hands when apologizing—a tendency that can be traced among several peoples—has precisely this meaning.

30 Following Petrażycki, I reconstruct authority as a jural phenomenon. See Fittipaldi 2016b.

31 Terminologically, I should use »Alter« only in the context of *jural* phenomena. Since guilt is a *moral* phenomenon, »Tertius« should« be used. I chose to use Alter for the sake of clarity.

I can now propose a reconstruction and formalization for the notions of *jural norm*, *jural obligation*, and *right*.

I propose to formalize differently the notion of *jural norm* depending on whether it is located in Alter's, Ego's, or Tertius's psyche.

If the jural norm is located in Alter—to whom from now on I will also refer to as »right-holder« without quotes[32]—it can be formulated as follows

$$(\neg b_{Ego}) \longrightarrow (ANGER_{Alter})\,(\neg b_{Ego})$$

that is, the not taking of behavior *b* on the part of Ego elicits anger in Alter at the not taking of behavior *b* on the part of Ego.[33]

If it is located in Ego, whom from now on I will also refer to as »jural duty-holder« without quotes, the jural norm can be formulated as follows:

$$(\neg b_{Ego}) \longrightarrow (RESIGNATION_{Ego})\,(ANGER_{Alter})\,(\neg b_{Ego}),$$

that is, the not taking of behavior *b* on the part of Ego elicits within Ego the resignation to the potential anger of Alter at the not taking of *b* on the part of Ego. This is what Ego's *acknowledgment* of Alter's jural expectation boils down to.

Finally, if it is located in Tertius, the jural norm can be formulated as follows:

$$(\neg b_{Ego}) \longrightarrow (IDENTIFICATION_{Tertius})\,(ANGER_{Tertius})(\neg b_{Ego})$$

,

that is, the not taking of behavior *b* on the part of Ego, due to Tertius' identification with Alter, elicits the anger of Tertius at Ego's behavior.

---

32 The reader should bear in mind though, that it is, (1) Alter's disposition to become angry and/or (2) Ego's jural resignation (see below) and/or (3) Tertius's vicarious anger (see below) *in the event Ego behaves in a certain way with regard to Alter* that cognitive-emotionally turn(s) Alter into a right-holder within the psyches of, respectively, Alter, Ego, and Tertius—*and not the other way around*.

33 $\neg b$ should be understood as any behavior possibly incompatible with the satisfaction of Alter's expectation (e.g., Ego's spending lots of money instead of saving to pay a debt she owes Alter). It should be also stressed that the emotion-elicitor is not the behavior per se but the behavior qua object of perception or representation.

In other words, in such cases, Tertius experiences anger *along with* or *in lieu of* Alter's anger. This is what Tertius's *vicarious anger* boils down to.

In each of these cases, we can say that the *norm according to which Ego should take the behavior b and Alter has the right that Ego take it* can exist in Alter, Ego, and/or Tertius, but, depending in whose psyche it is located, it boils down to a different jural emotion: anger, resignation, or vicarious anger.

As for the notions of *right, jural obligation,* and—for the sake of completeness—*jural prohibition,* they can be conceptualized as follows. A *right* is a possible—if in no way necessary—reification of a jural norm (see Fittipaldi 2021a and 2022a). In this chapter, though, to say that Alter has a right that Ego acts in a certain way is to be understood as meaning the existence of at least one of the three above described jural norms within, respectively, Alter's, Ego's, and/or Tertius's psyche.[34]

As for jural obligations and prohibitions, their conceptualization requires that we cease using »behavior« and distinguish between »action« in a strict sense and »abstention«. If we use x and $\neg x$ to refer to, respectively, an action and an abstention, we can formalize jural obligations and prohibitions, respectively, as follows (to save space, I confine myself solely to Alter's standpoint):

$$(\neg x_{Ego}) \longrightarrow (ANGER_{Alter})(\neg x_{Ego}),$$

that is, the abstention from x on the part of Ego elicits anger in Alter at the abstention from x on the part of Ego, and

34 The conceptualization proposed here *rules out moral rights* as a *contradictio in adiecto*. However, if all jural phenomena involve rights, not all rights involve jural phenomena. There also exist *agonistic rights,* that is, rights that boil down to (α) Alter's anger-backed expectation that Ego take a certain behavior but do *not* also involve (β) Alter's *distinct* anger-backed expectation that Ego resign herself to his anger should she not take the expected behavior. Due to space limitations, I cannot discuss this distinct expectation that makes it possible to distinguish between jural and agonistic rights. I confine myself to an example. In *vindicatory* cultures, if the avenge-taker (she) experienced the frustration of an expectation concerning a behavior of the prospective victim (he), she does not expect that he resignedly endures her revenge. Instead, in *punitive* cultures it is expected *both* that the victim does not take a certain behavior *and* that he resignedly endures the ensuing violence (punishment, atonement, expiation). For a discussion, see Fittipaldi 2022a (70), which elaborates on Kurczewski (1976).

$$(x_{Ego}) \longrightarrow (ANGER_{Alter})(x_{Ego})$$

that is, the taking of action x on the part of Ego elicits anger in Alter at the taking of x on the part of Ego.[35]

Thus far I have been dealing with rights concerning others' behaviors. But there exist also rights to one's own actions, such as rights of way or freedom of speech, as well as rights to one's own abstentions, such as the right to abstain from attending religious rites or a master's right not to feed her slaves (in some cultures).

I believe that such rights can formalized as follows.

If Alter's right to his own action or abstention is located within Ego, it can be, respectively, formalized as follows:

$$(x_{Alter}) \longrightarrow (RESIGNATION_{Ego})(x_{Alter})$$

$$(\neg x_{Alter}) \longrightarrow (RESIGNATION_{Ego})(\neg x_{Alter})$$

that is, Alter's taking action (or abstention from) x elicits within Ego the resignation to Alter's potentially taking (or not taking) of x.

If it is located within Alter, it can be, respectively, formalized as follows:

$$(\neg RESIGNATION_{Ego})(x_{Alter}) \longrightarrow (ANGER_{Alter})(\neg RESIGNATION_{Ego})(x_{Alter})$$

$$(\neg RESIGNATION_{Ego})(\neg x_{Alter}) \longrightarrow (ANGER_{Alter})(\neg RESIGNATION_{Ego})(\neg x_{Alter})$$

that is, Ego's not resignedly enduring Alter's taking (or not taking) x elicits anger in Alter at Ego's not resignedly enduring Alter's taking (or not taking) x.

Finally, if Alter's right to his own action or abstention is located within Tertius, it can be, respectively, formalized as follows:

---

[35] In this latter case, due to the cognitive salience of actions relative to abstentions, x_{Ego} may be construed as a *wrong* (to Alter), whereas in the former one x_{Ego} may be construed as the object of a *right* (of Alter).

$$(\neg RESIGNATION_{Ego})(x_{Alter}) \longrightarrow$$
$$(IDENTIFICATION_{Tertius})\,(ANGER_{Tertius})$$
$$(\neg RESIGNATION_{Ego})(x_{Alter})$$

$$(\neg RESIGNATION_{Ego})(\neg x_{Alter}) \longrightarrow$$
$$(IDENTIFICATION_{Tertius})\,(ANGER_{Tertius})$$
$$(\neg RESIGNATION_{Ego})(\neg x_{Alter})$$

that is, Ego's not resignedly enduring Alter's taking (or not taking) x, due to Tertius' identification with Alter, elicits Tertius' anger at Ego's not resignedly enduring Alter's taking (or not taking) x. Also in this case, Tertius' anger may occur either along with or in lieu of Alter's anger.

Prior to discussing the issue whether jural norms, rights, and jural obligations can be traced among non-human animals a point should be made.

Since it cannot in any way be taken for granted that Ego, Alter, and Tertius agree on *who is entitled to what from whom,* this reconstruction is strongly conflictualist, in that, it assumes that it may make perfect sense to speak of the existence of a right, despite the fact that *not* every interactant agrees on who has that right, to what that right is, and whether it at all exists. For a given right to exist, the belief in its existence of even only one single interactant suffices. This approach implies that divergent opinions are conducive to conflicts and in some cases to the emergence of *law,* understood as a a polythetic (social) phenomenon made up of adjudication, sources that are used to justify judges' rulings, and behaviors of people whose social role is to enforce those rulings.

We can now discuss the question whether non-human animals can have rights or jural obligations/prohibitions against each other.[36] If the questions whether non-human animals have jural norms and jural obligations/prohibitions toward each other seems to be an open one, the term »right« can be sometimes found in ethological literature. Here is an example from Wrangham:

36 The topic of rights ascribed to non-human animals by human animals is outside the scope of this chapter.

> Just as some people are more prone to reactive aggression than others, species also vary. Most, such as chimpanzees or wolves, are more prone to reactive aggression than humans are. The pattern has been well studied in animals. Reactive aggression is especially prominent among males fighting over status or mating *rights*. Normally, fights among animals end without injury, but if the stakes are high the competition can be severe. During a study of rut fighting among male pronghorn antelope, 12 percent of conflicts over mating *rights* to estrous females led to the death of one or both males. [Wrangham 2019, 27, emphases added]

As can be seen, Wrangham connects the notion of right to that of reactive aggression and, basically, my idea of connecting them draws on him. However, a few remarks are in order here.

First, since I conceptualize normative emotions as emotions that emerge or get reshaped by virtue of the child's interaction with her »godlike« caregiver, my conceptualization prevents me from using right in non-human contexts unless it can be shown that antelopes or chimpanzees undergo some form of socialization of their reactive aggression by virtue of the »godlike« manner they conceive of their caregiver; that which I regard as quite improbable.

However, since I believe that rights and jural obligations/prohibitions are the result[37] of the socialization of reactive aggression, I also believe that reactive aggression is the *immediate forerunner* of anger, and the mediate one of sense of entitlement and rights. If taken in this sense, I believe that what Wrangham calls »rights« could be understood (and, possibly, also referred to) as *proto-rights*.[38]

Second, it should be reiterated that my conceptualization does not require that to speak of the existence of a right in a system (comprised of at least Ego and Alter) Ego and Alter must agree on who is, respectively, the right- and the duty-holder, and to what exactly the right-holder is entitled to. However, such an agreement, or coordination is a common phenomenon in human societies, and it could be asked whether anything similar can be traced among non-human ones.

---

37 To be precise, I believe that rights and obligations are pseudo-concepts in the sense explained in Fittipaldi 2021a.

38 I am using »proto-«, not in its original Greek sense (»first«) but in the sense the prefix »fore« has in words like »forerunner«, »forebear«, »forefront«. The exact Greek term to be used is πρό, but this is not possible as in contemporary English the prefix *pro-* is mostly used in the sense of the Latin *pro*.

As a social theorist, it seems to me that such a phenomenon can be traced when in a chimpanzee community, after having defeated the previous alpha male, a male starts being regarded as an *alpha* by virtually all of its members (that which, besides the proto-right of monopoly over females, seems also to call into being the jural obligation to »greet« him with a pant-grunt [cf. Goodall 1986, 128]). This means that—unless some form of full-blown jural resignation can be shown to be present[39]—in such cases we can speak of *proto-resignation* within non-alpha males and conclude that, at least as far as the alpha males' proto-rights are concerned, a form of coordination involving the proto-resignation of the non-alpha males can be traced. Among other things, this *proto-resignation* appears to manifest itself in the manner non-alphas endure the alpha's quasi monopoly over females.

3.1.1.2 Indignation

As previously noted—unlike anger (and besides the cases of predation and territorality)—indignation may be perfectly gratuitous, that is, performed for its own sake, or—to put it in still another way—performed for the pure pleasure of inflicting suffering.

Indignation emerges as the result of the child learning that there are *types of circumstances* in which her caregiver tolerates or approves of her becoming aggressive, and so *even in the absence of any form of threat or frustration*. This is why I conceptualize indignation as *socialized proactive aggression*.

With respect to indignation, human animals employ the *cognitive salience* of the features or behaviors of some other animate beings (first and foremost, other human animals) as a *pretext* to carry out some form of aggression against them (including merely fantasized ones).[40] The salient features of those beings or behaviors may be the most diverse depending on the socialization of the child, including the secondary one. They may range from having unusual sexual behaviors to being and acting as a smart woman.

One may ask why human beings take other beings' cognitive salience as a pretext to be aggressive against them. In other words,

---

[39] By »full-blown resignation« I understand a jural resignation that is the result of some form of primary socialization.

[40] This hypothesis elaborates on Freud's »narcissism of small differences« (Freud 1929/1981, 114).

why do humans engage in *(moral) sadism*[41]? A possible hypothesis is that the development of proactive aggression among human animals is closely connected to conformism (cf. Wrangham 2019, 144), whether or not functional to some specific interest of the group.[42]

Be that as it may, what matters here are the following hypotheses: (1) that among human animals proactive aggression may be perfectly gratuitous and (2) that this form of aggression is capable of being socialized into what I stipulatively refer to as *indignation*.

What is key is that *indignation is not innate,* for it is *socialized proactive aggression*. A consequence is that, with their »godlike« prestige, caregivers can teach their children that gratuitous aggression can be safely exerted against certain targets—*but only them.*

An important component of my hypothesis is that, if a child's proactive aggression has been socialized to be directed solely towards certain targets (fascists, communists, homosexuals, supporters of a soccer team, people with a certain color of the skin, etc.), during the second socialization it can be *redirected* towards targets completely different from those against which it was tolerated or encouraged during primary socialization. Thus, for example, the child of communist may perfectly become a fascist whose socialized proactive aggression (i.e., indignation) is directed towards communists.

Indignation-backed norms can be formalized as follows:

$$\left(\neg b_{Ego}\right) \longrightarrow (INDIGNATION_{Tertius})\left(\neg b_{Ego}\right).$$

That is, the not taking of behavior *b* on the part of Ego elicits indignation in Tertius at the not taking of behavior of *b* on the part of Ego. In this case, no Alter is involved. Nor is any right-holder. This is why I regard indignation as a *moral* emotion. Here there can me no more than two types of interactant Ego and Tertius. Further, while jural, or anger backed, norms may be located in Ego (the duty-holder), in Alter (the right-holder), and Tertius (a bystander), indignation-backed norms can be located exclusively within Tertius' psyche—no corresponding normative emotion being possible within Ego).

---

[41] By »moral sadism« I understand a form of sadism that underwent socialization. I do not know whether unsocialized human animals are prone to what could be referred to as proto-moral sadism.

[42] It could be argued, though, that the repression of nonconformism, due to its enhancing groupishness is by definition functional to the persistence of groups over time.

Indignation-backed obligations and prohibitions can be formalized as follows:

$$\left(\neg x_{Ego}\right) \longrightarrow (INDIGNATION_{Tertius})\left(\neg x_{Ego}\right),$$

$$\left(x_{Ego}\right) \longrightarrow (INDIGNATION_{Tertius})\left(x_{Ego}\right).$$

To avoid misunderstandings, two phenomena should be now briefly discussed.

The first phenomenon is where Tertius *pretends* to be identifying with Alter's anger at something Ego did with regard to Alter. If Tertius is only taking as a *pretext* what Ego did to Alter, we are not dealing with a form anger, but with *full-blown indignation*. This is typically the case of those who participate in the lapidation of adulterers not because they sympathize with the cheated-on spouses, but simply for the »fun« of participating in the killing of a human being.[43]

The second phenomenon is revenge. Revenge may be caused by anger, indignation, or both of them, depending on the psychical experience of the revenge-taker.

For revenge to be a form of reactive aggression, it is not sufficient for the revenge-taker to have *previously* experienced a form of reactive aggression against the victim. It is necessary that the revenge-taker *still* experiences that emotion when carrying it out. If this is not the case, we are not dealing with anger-backed revenge, or *jural revenge*, but with a form of indignation-backed revenge, or *moral* revenge.

However, things may be more complex than that:

1. The decision to take revenge may be caused by an experience of reactive aggression;
2. Its planning may involve a form of proactive aggression; and
3. During its carrying out a re-experience of the reactive aggression that led to that decision may take place.

In such a case, I believe that we can still speak of a form of jural revenge or of a combination of a jural and moral revenge.

In general, I believe that most forms of revenge originate from an experience of reactive aggression, with the important exception,

43 It should be noted that indignation, unlike anger, mostly involves forms of imbalance of power (cfr. Wrangham 2019, 225).

though, of those cultures where revenge is the object of an obligation rather than a right. Think of the obligation to avenge a murdered kin in certain societies. This obligation may be a resignation- or an indignation-backed one depending on whether, in the event of non-revenge, Ego is resigned to endure Alter's[44] anger or Tertius has the disposition to become indignant.[45]

We can now ask, whether non-human animals are capable of indignation. As is known, such animals as chimpanzees patrol the borders of their group's territory and, if they encounter a lonely member of a neighboring group and there is a situation of imbalance of power, they kill that stranger prompted by a form of proactive aggression (cf., e.g., Wrangham 2019, 232). Unless such and similar behaviors can be shown to be the result of some form of socialization effected through the way the child conceives of her mother or other significant members in the community, my conceptualization implies that these are mere forms of *proto*-indignation.

3.1.1.3 Disgust

Paul Rozin and April E. Fanlon, by elaborating on some ideas of the Hungarian-American psychoanalyst Andras Angyal (1941), define disgust as »[r]evulsion at the prospect of (oral) incorporation of an offensive object« (Rozin & Fanlon 1987, 23). A first problem with this definition is that *the term »revulsion« already involves the idea of disgust*, and so we are not dealing with a well-formed definition. Further, the prospect of eating a *metal bolt* does indeed scare me but does not in any way produce the kind of revulsion that is typically involved by the prospect of incorporating, say, the *decaying corpse* of an animal. This is why *I would define disgust as a form of nausea caused by the perception or representation of something.*[46]

As much as anger and indignation—which have pre-socialized reactive and proactive aggression as their forerunners—also disgust appears to have its pre-socialized forerunner, namely, the less-than-three-year-old children's tendency to spit out bitter things (Herz 2012/13, 46); a tendency I refer to as proto-disgust.

---

44 Alter may exist only in Ego's psyche and be, for example, the ghost of person killed to whom Ego was related.

45 The obligation may also be a guilt-, shame-, or even pride-backed one. On these concepts, see below.

46 On the relation between disgust and the urge to vomit, see Herz 2012/13.

Proto-disgust gets reshaped by the caregiver and the result of this process—disgust proper—may be elicited by all sorts of things —including things insusceptible to incorporation (e.g., a behavior). Since I define as »normative emotions« the emotions that emerge or get reshaped by virtue of the »godlike« features the child ascribes to her caregiver, I do not distinguish between non-normative and normative disgust depending on whether it does or does not concern things capable of incorporation. Based on the conceptualization adopted here, also disgust elicited by certain foods[47] is a normative phenomenon, and there is no reason to distinguish between this form of disgust and the one elicited, say, by Nazis (cf. Sherman et al. n.d.). The only form of non-normative disgust is the above mentioned proto-disgust of less-than-three-year-old children.

The reasons why disgust, even if capable of being directed towards the most diverse objects, *is a human universal* are still debated and there is no room to discuss them here. Suffice here to say that this emotion seems to be related to human animals' awareness that they and their loved ones will someday die, and can be reconstructed as an emotion originating from our rejection of all reminders of our and our loved ones' inevitable death (cf. Herz 2012/13, especially 129–130).

Interestingly, normative disgust undergoes a *double socialization*. First, proto-disgust is turned into disgust proper (or normative disgust). Then, children are taught not to express their disgust in most, *though not all,* contexts. The result of this second socialization is that children learn that it is safe to express disgust only towards certain targets (e.g., excreta, Nazis, unfair behaviors). The result is that disgust works in a way similar to indignation, with the crucial difference, though, that indignation does not involve the urge to vomit.

I propose to formalize disgust-backed norms as follows:

$$\left(\neg b_{Ego}\right) \longrightarrow (DISGUST_{Tertius})\left(\neg b_{Ego}\right),$$

that is, the not taking of behavior *b* on the part of Ego elicits disgust in Tertius at the not taking of behavior of *b* on the part of Ego. Not even in this case is any Alter, or right-holder involved. This is why also disgust-backed norms must be characterized as *moral* emotions. I will briefly return to disgust below, when discussing shame.

---

47 Think of the disgust towards certain types of cheese many Asians have (Herz 2012/13, 2).

3.2 Guilt, shame, and pride

3.2.1. Why grouping them together

Guilt, shame, and pride are usually grouped together due to their being self-conscious emotions, in that they are hypothesized to presuppose self-awareness.[48] The reason why I group them together, though, is more basic. While anger proper, vicarious anger, indignation, and disgust are located either in Alter (the right-holder) or in Tertius (a possible bystander),[49] guilt, shame, and pride are all located in Ego (the duty-holder).[50] I discuss them in this order.

3.2.1.1 Guilt

From the psychoanalytical perspective adopted here, guilt starts emerging when the child becomes aware that she caused to her caregiver some form of pain or distress. This means that the emergence of guilt presupposes the innate ability of the child to *empathetically*—though not necessarily sympathetically[51]—understand the presence of certain emotions in others. Thus, empathy can be regarded as a form of proto-guilt.

The child loves and fears her »godlike« caregiver and is also terrified of losing the love of a person on whom she depends entirely (see Section 2, on *respect*). If, by empathizing with him, she realizes that he is experiencing some pain or distress due to something she did, she may become terrified at the idea of losing his love. Guilt is here understood as the *unconscious re-experience* of this terrifying experience. What is key is that in the case of guilt a form of unconscious re-experience is involved, which re-experience turns proto-guilt both:

---

48 The reconstruction of guilt and shame offered here elaborates on Lewis (1971) and Tangney & Dearing (2002). The reconstruction of pride elaborates on Sandler (1960).

49 To be sure, above I discussed *jural resignation*, which is also located in Ego. I discussed it above for the sake of clarity.

50 An exception is contagious shame, which—due to space limitations—is not discussed here.

51 By »empathy« I understand the ability to *understand* others' feelings *without* necessarily experiencing anything similar to them, while by »sympathy« I understand empathy *along with* the ability to have such experiences.

α .into a full-blown normative emotion and
β .into a more painful emotion than *mere regret*.

This is so because—unlike guilt—regret does *not*:

α′ require socialization,
β′ or involve the mentioned re-experience.

Prior to formalizing guilt-backed norms, it should be pointed out that—just as in the case of the other normative emotions discussed here—once proto-guilt has turned into full-blown normative guilt, it can be experienced also toward animate beings *other than* one's caregiver.

Based on this conceptualization, a guilt-backed norm can be conceptualized as follows:

$$\left(\neg b_{Ego}\right) \longrightarrow \left(GUILT_{Ego}\right)\left(\neg b_{Ego}\right)$$

That is, the not taking of behavior *b* on the part of Ego elicits within Ego guilt at her not taking of behavior *b*. Similarly, guilt-backed obligations and prohibitions can, respectively, be formalized as follows:

$$\left(\neg x_{Ego}\right) \longrightarrow \left(GUILT_{Ego}\right)\left(\neg x_{Ego}\right)$$

$$\left(x_{Ego}\right) \longrightarrow \left(GUILT_{Ego}\right)\left(x_{Ego}\right)$$

We can conclude this Section by asking whether non-human animals can experience guilt. My hypothesis is that the forerunner of guilt is empathy, as distinct from sympathy.[52] If some animals are, probably, capable of proto-guilt, they are not capable of experiencing normative guilt, unless they can be shown to experience their caregiver in the way monotheisms conceive of the One God.

If non-human animals are probably incapable of experiencing normative guilt, they may be capable of experiencing what I refer to as *para-guilt* (from the Ancient Greek preposition »παρά«, used here in the sense of »parallel to«). To introduce this hypothesis I avail myself of Frans de Waal's discussion of Konrad Lorenz's hypothesis that the latter's dog Bully once experienced a form of guilt. Lorenz related that

---

52 Empathy, or proto-guilt, enables one's to survive in a social environment without having any concern for others' well-being by simply calculating in advance their possible reactions to one's own actions. Its non-normative nature is apparent.

Bully had accidentally bit his hand when he was trying to break up a dog fight in which he (Bully) was involved. Lorenz did not reprimand him. On the contrary, he immediately attempted to reassure him (by petting him). This notwithstanding, according to Lorenz, Bully suffered a nervous breakdown. For days he was virtually paralyzed and uninterested in food. He lied on the rug breathing shallowly and sometimes produced sounds similar to sighs. Further, for weeks he remained extremely subdued.

According to de Waal, instead of reconstructing Bully's behavior as a manifestation of guilt, it would be more appropriate to hypothesize that »he expected punishment, perhaps, even expulsion from the pack« (de Waal 1996, 106).

As noted previously, guilt can be reconstructed as an adolescent's or adult's *unconscious re-experience* of her infantile dread of losing her caregiver's love or simply—pun intended—care. Once learned, this emotion can be experienced even when one's caregiver(s) has long passed away and toward people completely unrelated to her. This phenomenon involves a mechanism psychoanalysts refer to as *transference*, that is, *the process by which Self* (usually, but not necessarily a patient) *displaces onto Other feelings, ideas, etc., which derive from previous significant figures in Self's life* (cf. Rycroft 1968/1995: 185). Guilt involves such a displacement.

Now, if in the relation with their masters dogs effect a displacement from the pack to the master, we are dealing with a phenomenon similar to (though not identical with) guilt, in that, even if dogs' attitudes towards the pack are probably quite different from those of the helpless child toward her caregiver, this notwithstanding we are dealing with an emotion that affects the dog's behavior due to its relation to a being (or a set of beings) that is somewhat perceived as *significant* (and superordinate): the pack. This is why, in this case, I believe we can speak of para-guilt.

3.2.1.2 Shame

Along with the inhibition of his child's aggressiveness, one of the first things the caregiver tries to teach her is how to deal with her bodily wastes, saliva, bolus, etc. This aspect of primary socialization is often referred to as »toilet training«, but this term is too narrow as it does not cover, for example, the tabooization of eructation. Other scholars used such terms as »sphincter morality« (Ferenczi 1925, 379) or »habituation into pureness [*Reinlichkeitsangewöhnung*]« (Müller-Braunschweig 1922, 250). As a result of this form of socialization the child learns to experience what in many languages we refer to as shame.

Since the elicitors of shame vary dramatically across cultures, I believe that instead of characterizing it based on its elicitors, it is better to characterize it based on its origin, whose features—according to the psychoanalytic approach adopted here—perpetuate themselves into adolescence and adulthood.

My hypothesis is that shame amounts to the experience of being disgusting to other people and emerges due to the caregiver's displays of disgust with regard to certain activities or excreta of the child. In other words, the experience of shame may be reconstructed as the unconscious re-experience of the child's experience of being disgusting to her »godlike« caregiver.[53] Quite literally—at least in many cultures—, to be ashamed amounts to unconsciously experiencing oneself like the bodily waste »par excellence« in the eyes of one's God.[54]

When children become adolescents and then adults, this experience—or, to be precise, re-experience—may be elicited by a variety of behaviors or events, which may be completely unrelated to bodily wastes or organic matter resembling or reminding of decaying corpses. Examples can range from making a solecism to wearing an outmoded tie.

The manner in which shame-backed norms, obligations, and prohibitions can be formalized is identical with the way I have formalized guilt-backed norms, obligations, and prohibitions.

$$(\neg b_{Ego}) \longrightarrow (SHAME_{Ego})(\neg b_{Ego})$$

$$(\neg x_{Ego}) \longrightarrow (SHAME_{Ego})(\neg x_{Ego})$$

53 Displays of disgust may occur in a completely unintentional manner. A problem with this conjecture could be that many children interpret disgust faces as expressions of anger (Widen & Russell 2010). The theory proposed in text would be falsified if it could be shown that children are capable of developing shame before developing their ability distinguish between disgust and anger faces. On the role of disgust faces in the socialization of children, see also Lewis 1992 (110).

54 To be sure, in certain cultures this experience may even be conscious. In some languages (e.g., Italian), to report one's experience of shame, sentences that should be literally translated as »I felt [like] a s**t« are used (»Mi sono sentito una m***a«).

$$(x_{Ego}) \longrightarrow (SHAME_{Ego})(x_{Ego})$$

Finally, it can be asked whether shame can be found in non-human animals. I hypothesize it cannot, unless it can be shown that they can experience normative disgust and that non-human mothers use this emotion (also inadvertently) when interacting with their children.

3.2.1.3 Pride

If guilt and shame can be regarded as internal *negative* sanctions that motivate behaviors aimed at averting them, pride can be regarded as an internal *positive* sanction that motivates behaviors aimed at experiencing it.

As noted repeatedly, my approach is premised on the hypothesis that the child conceives of her caregiver in the manner monotheisms conceive of the One God. Consequently, the most exciting experience for a child is to believe to be like her »godlike« caregiver or to meet his expectations (especially if these latter are themselves pride-backed). Pride can be reconstructed as the unconscious re-experience of that experience during adolescence and then adulthood.

Once we learn to experience pride, it can be elicited by the most diverse accomplishments, including ones our caregivers know nothing about or they would disapprove of. For example, the child of staunch atheists, during second socialization may become a believer who proudly practices painful penitential practices to be closer to the sufferings undergone by Jesus. Also in such cases (above, Section 3.2.1), a form of transference is at work (from the caregiver to the peer group).

I believe that much of what is referred to as »sense of duty« can be traced to pride-backed norms. One may hypothesize that at least some acts of heroism are performed out of the narcissistic wish to experience pride.[55]

Pride-backed norms, obligations, and prohibitions can be formalized as follows:

---

[55] Interestingly, often these acts are understated by suggesting they are nothing but the discharge of one's duty.

$$(b_{\text{Ego}}) \longrightarrow (PRIDE_{\text{Ego}})(b_{\text{Ego}})$$

$$(x_{\text{Ego}}) \longrightarrow (PRIDE_{\text{Ego}})(x_{\text{Ego}})$$

$$(\neg x_{\text{Ego}}) \longrightarrow (PRIDE_{\text{Ego}})(\neg x_{\text{Ego}})$$

Also in this case, we are to ask whether non-human animals can have pride-backed norms, obligations, and prohibitions. Unless it can be demonstrated that, when still dependent on their caregivers, they experience them as having »godlike« features, this hypothesis cannot be made.

4. Conclusion

In this chapter, I have endeavored to show that norms, rights, and obligations, can be naturalized if understood as couplings of (α) normative emotions and (β) perceptions/representations of behaviors or states of affairs.

Definitional circularity has been avoided by defining normative emotions as the emotions that emerge or get reshaped due to children's ascription to their caregivers of the features that monotheisms ascribe to the One God, provided some of those features unconsciously characterize those emotions also during adolescence and adulthood.

I also hypothesized that some normative emotions have forerunners traceable among non-human animals, some of which may prompt them to act in ways that closely resemble human normative behavior. These forerunners are: proto-anger, proto-resignation, proto-indignation. Further, I attempted to clarify in what way it can make sense to speak of proto-rights and jural proto-obligations. Finally, I hypothesized that among some animals transference mechanisms may be at work, which mechanisms make it possible to speak, not of *forerunners* of certain human normative emotions, but of phenomena *parallel* to them: para-guilt.

If this approach can be accepted, one of its main corollaries is that, *whenever we speak of norms, rights, and obligations (especially among human animals), we must always ask which normative emotions back- or, more precisely, constitute them.*

Among other things, this means that we cannot confine ourselves to distinguishing between shame and guilt cultures. We must always investigate to what extent different normative emotions play a motivational role in different societies and with regard to what types of behavior.

The normative emotions—let alone the non-normative ones—that cause certain patterns of behaviors may be the most diverse. In certain societies, certain behaviors may be taken overwhelmingly because social actors fear the anger or indignation of other social actors. In such cases the only normative emotions that play a role are those within Alter and Tertius—Ego acting solely out of fear, a non-normative (or selfish) emotion. In other societies, instead a role may be played by the desire to avoid the experience of jural resignation, whether or not combined with guilt (or shame). In this case all normative emotions are located in Ego.

Further, we should bear in mind that within the very same society different types of behavior may be caused by different normative emotions. For example, certain sets of behaviors may be caused by the desire to avoid the experience of shame or guilt, others by that of avoiding jural resignation, and still others simply by the non-normative desire of avoiding the angry reactions of others.

As for the notion of *normative behavior*—as distinct from that of *non-normative behavior*—, it can be re-conceptualized as a behavior *emotionally consonant* with some normative emotion. For example, Ego acts normatively if she takes action x in order *not* to resignedly endure Alter's reaction should she not take x or (β) if she *resignedly* endures his reaction should she not take x.[56]

In tables (1) and (2), I summarize the various notions of norm, right, and obligation, expounded here.

[56] More on the difficult problems connected to the notion of »emotional consonance« as used here can be found in Fittipaldi 2022b.

Table 1. Naturalization of norms according to which one should (or ought to) perform an action and possibly someone else is entitled to it

Norm* according to which Ego *should* (or has the *obligation* to) take action x (and possibly Alter has the *right* that Ego take it)		
Participant within which the norm, right, or obligation is located: Ego and/or Alter and/or Tertius		
EGO	**ALTER**	**TERTIUS**
Ego's *resignation* in the event of Alter's anger at Ego's *not* taking action x and Alter's anger at Ego's non-resignation at Alter's anger at Ego's not taking action x		
Ego's *guilt* in the event of Ego's *not* taking action x		
Ego's *shame* in the event of Ego's *not* taking action x		
Ego's *pride* in the event of Ego's taking action x		
	Alter's *anger* at Ego's not taking action x and at Ego's non-resignation at Alter's anger at Ego's not taking action x	
		Tertius' *identification with Alter's anger (vicarious anger)* in the event of Ego's not taking action x and Ego's non-resignation to Alter's anger at Ego's not taking action x
		Tertius' *indignation* in the event of Ego's not taking action x
		Tertius' *disgust* in the event of Ego's not taking action x
		Tertius' *contagious shame* in the event of Ego's not taking action x
*Jural phenomena—as distinct from moral ones—are underlined.		

Table 2. Naturalization of norms according to which one can (or has the right to) perform an action and possibly someone else has the obligation to endure it

Norm according to which Alter _can_ (or has the _right_ to) take action _x_ (and possibly Alter has the _obligation_ to endure it)*		
Participant within which the norm, right, or obligation is located: Ego and/or Alter and/or Tertius		
EGO	**ALTER**	**TERTIUS**
Ego's *resignation* in the event of Alter's taking action x and Alter's anger at Ego's non-resignation at Alter's taking action x		
Ego's *guilt* in the event of Ego's non-resignation to Tertius's taking action x		
Ego's *shame* in the event of Tertius's non-resignation to Alter's taking action x		
Ego's *pride* in the event of Ego's resignation to Tertius taking action x		
	Alter's *anger* in the event of Ego's non-resignation to Alter's taking action x and Alter's anger at Ego's non-resignation to Alter's anger at Ego's non-resignation to Alter's taking x	
		Tertius' *identification with Alter's anger (vicarious anger)* in the event of Ego's non-resignation to Alter's taking action x and of Alter's anger at Ego's non-resignation to Alter's anger at Ego's non-resignation to Alter's taking x
		Tertius' *indignation* in the event of Ego's non-resignation to Alter's taking action x

	Tertius' *disgust* in the event of Ego's non-resignation to Alter's taking action x
	Tertius' *contagious shame* in the event of Ego's non-resignation to Alter's taking action x
*Jural phenomena—as distinct from moral ones—are underlined.	

Two final remarks are in order here.[57]

First, it could be asked under what circumstances this conceptualization should be rejected. My answer is that it should be rejected if the hypotheses on which it rests should be (provisionally) regarded as falsified.[58] A very basic form of falsification would be the discovery of a feral child who is able to experience normative emotions. I am aware that such an answer may appear unsatisfactory to many. But I am not a natural scientist. I am a social epistemologist and as such I see as part of my job to formulate conjectures aimed at naturalizing concepts that are taken for granted by empirical scientists without asking what empirical phenomena are behind them. Here I have discussed such concepts as those of »norm«, »right«, »obligation«. My hope is that my proposals will stimulate the fantasy of empirical scientists and prompt them to invent ways to falsify the conjectures on which these conceptualizations are premised.

Second, even if my conceptualization of normative emotions should get partly or entirely falsified, the problem I raise in this chapter would be here to stay: In what way—if any—do primary and secondary socialization influence such innate features of human animals as reactive and proactive aggression, disgust toward bitter substances, or empathy?

57 I wish to thank again Sergei Talanker for helping me to realize the importance of these two issues.

58 No theory can be ultimately verified or falsified with certainty. However, falsificationism has certain advantages over verificationism that cannot be discussed here.

References

Angyal, Andras, 1941. Disgust and related aversions. *Journal of Abnormal and Social Psychology*, 36: 393–412.

Bovet, Pierre, 1917. Le respect: essai de psychologie morale. *Revue de Théologie et de Philosophie*, 5, 2: 204–222.

—, 1925/1928. *Le sentiment religieux et la psychologie de l'enfant*. English translation *The Child's Religion*. London & Toronto (ON): Dent & Sons.

De Waal, Frans, 1996. *Good Natured: The Origins of Right and Wrong in Humans and Other Animals*. Cambridge (MA) & London: Harvard University Press.

DSM-5, 2013. *Diagnostic and Statistical Manual of Mental Disorders*. American Psychiatric Publishing: Washington (DC) & London.

Ferenczi, Sándor 1925. Psychoanalysis of sexual habits. *The International Journal of Psycho-Analysis*, 6: 372–404.

Fittipaldi, Edoardo, 2016a. *Introduction: Continental Legal Realism*. In Enrico Pattaro & Corrado Roversi (eds.), *Legal Philosophy in the Twentieth Century: The Civil Law World. Tome 2: Main Orientations and Topics*. Dordrecht: Springer.

—, 2016b. *Leon Petrażycki's Theory of Law*. In Enrico Pattaro & Corrado Roversi (eds.), *Legal Philosophy in the Twentieth Century: The Civil Law World, Tome 2: Main Orientations and Topics*. Dordrecht: Springer.

—, 2021a. Reducing Norms to Superegoic Emotions. *Etica & Politica / Ethics & Politics*, 23, 2021, 2: 283–307.

—, 2021b. *On Searle's Derivation and Its Relation to Constitutive Rules: A Social Scientist's Perspective*. In Paolo Di Lucia & Edoardo Fittipaldi, Revisiting Searle on Deriving »Ought« from »Is«. Cham: Palgrave Macmillan

—, 2022a. *Norma. Una concettualizzazione per la sociologia del diritto e le altre scienze sociali*. Milan: LED.

—, 2022b. From Norms to Normative Behaviors. *L'Ircocervo*, 21, 2: 233–249.

—, 2023. *Petrażycki's Puzzle of Jural Emotions: Bridging the Psychological Theory of Law with Modern Social and Psychological Sciences*. In Edoardo Fittipaldi & A. Javier Treviño (eds.), *Leon Petrażycki: Law, Emotions, Society*. Routledge: New York & London.

Freud, Sigmund, 1929/1981. *Das Unbehagen in der Kultur*. English translation *Civilization and Its Discontents* in Sigmund Freud (James Strachey ed.), *The Future of an Illusion, Civilization and Its Discontents* and *Other Works*. London: The Hogarth Press and The Institute of Psychoanalysis.

—, 1932/1981. *Neue Folge der Vorlesungen zur Einführung in die Psychoanalyse*. English translation *New Introductory Lectures on Psycho-Amnalysis* in Sigmund Freud (James Strachey ed.), *New Introductory Lectures on Psycho-Analysis* and *Other Works*. London: The Hogarth Press and The Institute of Psychoanalysis.

Gibbs, Jack P. 1968. *Norms. II. The Study of Norms*. In David L. Sills & Robert K. Merton (eds.), *The International Encyclopaedia of Social Sciences*, vol. 11, London & New York: The Macmillan Co. & The Free Press.

Goodall, Jane, 1986. *The Chimpanzees of Gombe: Patterns of Behavior*. Cambridge (MA) & London: The Belknap Press of Harvard University Press.

Haidt, Jonathan, 2002. *The Moral Emotions*. In Klaus Scherer, Richard Davidson, & H. Hill Goldsmith, *Handbook of Affective Sciences*. Oxford: Oxford University Press.

Herz, Rachel, 2012/13. *That's Disgusting: Unraveling the Mysteries of Repulsion*. New York & London: W.W. Norton & Company.

Kurczewski, Jacek, 1976. *Ambiguous Reciprocity*. The Polish Sociological Bulletin, 2: 5–16.

Lewis, Helen B. 1971. *Shame and Guilt in Neurosis*. New York: International Universities Press.

Lewis, Michael, 1992. *Shame. The Exposed Self*. New York: The Free Press.

Müller-Braunschweig, Carl, 1922. Psychoanalytische Gesichtspunkte zur Psychogenese der Moral, insbesondere des moralischen Aktes. *Imago*, 7: 237–250.

Pattaro, Enrico, 2005. *The Law and the Right: A Reappraisal of the Reality that Ought to Be*. Dordrecht: Springer.

Petrażycki, Leon, 1908/1933. *Vvedenie v izučenie prava i nravstvennosti. Osnovy èmocional'noj psihologii*. Abridged translation of the 3rd ed. *Methodologie des Rechts und der Moral. Zugleich eine neue allgemeine logische Lehre von der Bildung der allgemeinen Begriffe und Theorien*. Paris: Sirey.

Petrażycki, Leon 1909–1910. *Teorija prava i gosudarstva v sviazi s teoriej nravstvennosti*. Saint Petersburg: Ekateringofskoe Pečatnoe Delo.

Piaget, Jean, 1932/1948. *Le jugement moral chez l'enfant*. English translation *The Moral Judgement of the Child*. Glencoe (IL): The Free Press.

Pinker, Steven, 2011. *The Better Angels of Our Nature: Why Violence Has Declined*. New York: Penguin Books.

Rozin, Paul, & April E. Fanlon, 1987. *A Perspective on Disgust*. 94, 1: 23–41.

Rycroft, Charles, 1968/1995. *A Critical Dictionary of Psychoanalysis*. 2nd ed. London: Penguin Books.

Sandler, Joseph, 1960. *On the Concept of SuperEgo*. The Psychoanalytic Study of the Child, 15 (3): 128–162.

Sherman, Gary D., Jonathan Haidt, & James A. Coan, n.d. *The Psychophysiology of Moral Disgust: Throat Tightness and Heart Rate Deceleration*. Unpublished manuscript.

Tangney, June P., & Ronda L. Dearing, 2002. *Shame and Guilt*. London: The Guildford Press.

Tomasello, Michael, 2019. *Becoming Human: A Theory of Ontogeny*. London & Cambridge (MA): The Belknap Press of Harvard University Press.

Widen, Sherri C., & James A. Russell, 2010. The »Disgust Face« Conveys Anger to Children. *Emotion*, 10(4): 455–466.

Wrangham, Richard, 2017/2018. Two types of aggression in human evolution. *Proceedings of the National Academy of Sciences of the United States of America*, available at https://www.pnas.org/content/115/2/245 (accessed May 28th, 2021).

—, 2019. *The Goodness Paradox: The Strange Relationship between Virtue and Violence*. New York: Pantheon Books.

John J. Drummond

The Normativity of Norms

1. Introduction

The term »norm« in ordinary usage is equivocal.[1] We speak, for example, of statistical norms that are sometimes used to specify the so-called normal. We might say that it is the norm—that is, it is normal—over an entire population that the workday falls between the hours of 6:00 am and 8:00 pm, while knowing full well that this is not true for a large subset of the population. This use of »norm« approaches the sense of »most« or »the majority.« Beyond the statistical point, however, norms in this sense have no practical, moral, or legal effect. I put aside this sense of the term »norm.«

The term »norm« is also used in relation to social practices of various sorts. In these contexts, norms are the »unplanned result of individual interactions« (Bicchieri, Muldoon, and Sontuoso 2018) that manifest themselves as conventional rules, patterns, or standards for how one goes about performing a task, interacting with others, or filling a role. Social norms guide, control, or regulate conduct but while now having practical effect, they have no moral or legal effect. They serve primarily to provide a measure of order in and predictability to our social relationships and to contribute to the cooperative functioning of a community. Although the norms and expectations accompanying them might be wholly arbitrary (and, perhaps, even immoral), we wish to conform to the expectations of others, and they wish to conform to our expectations.

Although not themselves moral principles or laws, norms are sometimes derived from or related to laws or moral principles. For

1 This paper's first incarnation was a lecture presented at a conference on »Rethinking the Sources of Normativity in Ethics," held (virtually) at Friedrich-Alexander-Universität Erlangen-Nürnberg on March 25–26, 2021. I am grateful to the participants in the conference, especially Karsten Stueber, Alessio Rotundo, and Steven Crowell, for helpful remarks on the original version of the paper.

example, a provision of the Constitution of the United States requires that the President »shall from time to time give to the Congress Information of the State of the Union, and recommend to their Consideration such Measures as [s]he shall judge necessary and expedient« (Art. 2, sect. 3). Various norms complement, in the sense of complete, our understanding of this provision: It is now called (since 1946) the »State of the Union Address«; it is presented to the Congress near the beginning of the calendar year; since 1913, it is delivered orally and in person to a joint session of House of Representatives and the Senate rather than as a written submission. Other norms supplement, rather than complement, our understanding of Presidential behavior. It does not follow from any constitutional provision, but it is the norm that the White House have a Press Secretary, that the Press Secretary hold regular briefings for the press, that the President occasionally hold press conferences, and that the President and Press Secretary treat reporters respectfully.

Why do we conform to norms, if we do? One view is that they assist us in making sense of our situation and gaining for us the approval of others. So, when setting a table, we put the fork to the left and the knife to the right, thereby gaining approval from our mothers and grandmothers. Another view is that the »force«—the »bindingness«—of a social norm flows from the fact that adherence to it allows an agent to avoid public rebuke, sanction, or reprisal for having violated the norm, thereby preserving her good-standing in the community as one who is evaluated by the community as behaving appropriately. This has the practical effect of endowing the norms with a social significance that serves to hold us accountable to one another. Such social accountability ensures social tranquility from the point of view of both the agent and the community and further promotes shared values and cultural identity. In such a context, agents acquire »a second-order disposition to monitor one's behavior for its normative appropriateness« (Stueber 2005, 308) and the second-order disposition is actualized only in situations wherein »the appropriateness of one's behavior becomes an issue« (Stueber 2005, 319–20).

Because norms are not laws, however, there is often no penalty at all for violating them. Given the view that social norms arise in human interactions, as the shape of the interaction changes, so too can the norms. Indeed, it is frequently an expectation that norms will evolve over time as new factors shape human interaction. Something new—say, no work-emails on weekends—can »become the norm.«

A third view claims we conform to norms because we experience them as binding, as obligating us in a certain manner. But what accounts for this view? While many norms, such as those mentioned above, are merely conventional—even arbitrary—rules or standards, some norms seem to have a more law-like character. What should we say, for example, about a normative science like logic? Logical norms—indeed, we call them »logical laws«—are rooted in the nature of rational experience itself, and their bindingness is inseparable from the ends of reason. Does this fact about the epistemic norms of logic provide a clue for understanding practical norms that do not have the law-like character of logical norms? Why do we experience such practical norms as binding, if we do? This, then, is the question I shall explore: What accounts for the normativity of norms *for me* or *for us,* that is, what accounts for their bindingness, the sense that norms—or at least some of them—obligate us?

I will address this question within a framework established by a distinction between epistemic and practical norms, and with regard to practical norms, between first- and second-order norms. I shall discuss how these different norms come to have the status of norms and what accounts for their normativity. As a preview of the position, I suggest that the normativity of norms is rooted in the structures and goods—the values, if you will—inherent in the structures of rational experience itself. Chief among these structures is intentionality, the mind's directedness to the world, and chief among these goods is truthfulness in a sense I will characterize as I proceed.

2. Epistemic norms

The *telos* at which experiences—indeed, all of reason in its broadest sense—aim is truthfulness, that is, (1) cognizing, judging, and theorizing entities as they are, (2) having appropriate affective and evaluative attitudes toward those entities, and (3) acting rightly in response to and on the basis of our truthful cognitions and attitudes. I use the term »entity« broadly; it encompasses existent things, states of affairs, parts, properties, relations, and events, but also possible objects, fictional objects, ideal objects, and so forth—the kinds of things the experience of which is tied to our experience of actual (i.e., real, spatio-temporal) entities (Crane 2001, 337; Drummond 2012, 115). And I use the term »truthfulness," rather than »truth," in order to emphasize that a notion of correctness ranges across all the forms of reason: truth in the cognitive-theoretical domain, appropriateness in the axiological domain, and rightness in the practical domain (Husserl 2014, 278; Drummond 2010, 443; 2022, 125). Epistemic norms, consequently, range across all the domains of reason.

Any single experience is essentially a complex of intentions, at least some of which are empty intentions in which an entity or a part or aspect of the entity to which the experience is directed is intended or meant in its absence. This empty intention might, for example, be a supposition about a place I have never visited or a distant memory of a no longer living person. The experiential telos is realized in another experience (or phase of the same experience) that fulfills the empty intendings by way of perceptually apprehending the entity (part or aspect) in its bodily presence or in an experience having a perceptual basis. So, I might visit that place and see that it is as I supposed. Or I might work my memory to bring back the details of the person I was trying to remember so that I can envision her, or I might rely on a picture of the person (which is a rather complicated form of fulfillment).

This relation between empty and fulfilling intentions obtains even in the case of intuitive experiences such as the mere perception of, say, a house. Standing in a particular place, I visually experience the house as a three-dimensional entity having its own position in space. I directly and sensuously experience, however, only a particular, perspectival appearance of the house—perhaps its façade. But I do not perceive only the façade; I perceive the house. My perceiving also intends the sides and rear of the house, even though they are not at the moment directly presented in the way the façade is. While looking at the directly presented façade, in other words, I envision, but do not directly see, the other sides and the rear of the house; they are emptily intended. I now commence to walk around the house, and this movement generates other appearances of the house from different perspectives and with different foci. The house is perceptually present to me as the identical thing presented in the manifold of appearances generated as I walk around it, and these new appearances present directly or fail to present directly what I envisioned when looking at the house from the front.

Certain conditions must be met for the temporally extended perception of the house to be veridical. There must, first of all, be an agreement of sense, at least at the generic level, among the appearances. Imagine the façade of the house is red brick. Our envisioning other sides of the house might anticipate that they too will be made of red brick. As we move around the house, however, we see that the sides and rear are white clapboard. The appearances disagree with regard to the species and color of the building materials, but they are in agreement in both cases with respect to genus. This generic similarity is sufficient to constitute agreement of sense.

Whereas the appearances are joined by a generic similarity as two appearances of the house, my bodily movements are not generically similar to the perceptual appearances generated by my movements. The connection between my movements and the appearances is of an entirely different sort; it is a functional connection (Husserl 1997, 143). The changes in the flow of appearances are a *function* of the changes in my bodily position relative to the house. As I move, the contents at one margin of the visual field move out of the field, the contents previously at the center of the field move to that margin, the contents at the other margin of the field move to the center, and new contents enter at the now vacated margin. This movement with its rule-governed consequences generates the manifold of appearances in which the identical house is present to me in the experience. Herein—in the generic agreement of sense and the perceiver's bodily movement functionally motivating new appearances of the entity that fulfill the envisionings in prior phases of the experience—are found the norms governing the unfolding of temporally extended, veridical perceptions.[2]

Perceptions can, of course, fail. Consider the example of seeing a puddle of water on a highway on a hot, sunny day. As we approach the puddle, its apparent size diminishes, and it might reappear farther down the road. This sequence of appearances violates a norm proper to the functional connection between bodily movements and the flow of appearances. The norm is that as we approach a thing, it occupies a larger portion of our visual field. The facts that the apparent puddle on

[2] Husserl gives numerous accounts of the functional, motivational connection between kinaesthetic processes and determined series of appearances. The most detailed, some of which we explicate here, are in Husserl 1997, 131–245. Brief accounts can be found in Husserl 1989, 60–63, 128–29, 227–32; 2001, 48–52, 151–52; 1973, 83–85, 104. See also Drummond 1979.

the road diminishes in size and spontaneously relocates itself indicate to us that the apparent puddle on the road is illusory—it is in fact a mirage—and the perception is non-veridical.

The norms governing functional connection between bodily movements and appearances and the agreement of sense between the directly sensed appearance, the elapsed appearances, and the fulfilled envisionings of yet-to-come appearances through the course of a temporally extended perception are proto-logical. They are proto-logical insofar as they govern the relations among senses, the different senses of the thing in its varied appearances. Perception provides the stuffs out of which judgments are made, and the proto-logical norms are continuous with the logical norms that govern judgments. Logical norms, in turn, govern (1) well-formed propositions, (2) the consistency- and inferential-relations among well-formed propositions, and (3) the evidential confirmation of propositions (Husserl 1969, §§ 12–16). The norms governing the consistency- and inferential relations among well-formed propositions concern deductive validity and non-deductive strength, and the norms governing the evidential confirmation of the premises of an argument concern soundness and cogency. This last notion of evidential confirmation, which is crucial to normative logic as a theory of science, Husserl discusses under the headings of fulfillment, fulfilling intentions, intuition, and evidence.

Experience involves a striving for fulfillment, and rational experience requires evidence. Evidence is not properly to be understood as the providing of reasons in support of some claim or viewpoint. Providing reasons of this sort appeals to a secondary sense of reason as reasoning. The primary sense of reason is »evidencing« the truth of something. To evidence something is to experience the agreement between what is merely meant and what is intuitively given or grounded in an intuitive givenness (Husserl 2014, 287–88); it is to experience a fulfilling intention, an intention that fulfills the empty intending of the object. In the case of a cognitive judgment, for example, evidence is the act in which I am aware of the »congruence« or »coincidence« (*Deckung*) between the sense of a mere assertion and the sense of the directly intuited state of affairs (Husserl 2001b, 2:263–64; 2001a, 146–47). The intuited sense can be, as it were, laid over the asserted sense such that we recognize their coincidence, their identity.

This notion of reason, as noted above, is not restricted to cognitive-theoretical experience. It pertains as well to the axiological and practical domains. Axiological reason and practical reason are not rational in just the way cognitive-theoretical reason is, but they are rational in their own ways. They have their own »logics« and their own form of fulfillment. For all the forms of reason, the aim of experiential life is to secure intuitively grounded evidences in which entities are directly present to the subject and experienced in a manner that fulfills our suppositions about the way things are.

In the axiological sphere, evaluative correctness is evidently attained when the feeling or emotion disclosing the value-attribute is appropriate. A feeling or emotion is appropriate when the underlying non-axiological properties of the entity to which the feeling or emotion is a response are correctly apprehended, when the feeling or emotive response is fitting—that is, psychologically well motivated—in both type and intensity, and when the value-attribute disclosed is epistemically justified by the non-axiological features of the entity (Drummond 2017, 154–63). An experience satisfying these conditions is an evidenced axiological insight. Fear, for example, is appropriate when I correctly apprehend an entity as potentially causing me or someone near to me physical or psychological harm, my fearing the entity is not exaggerated in its intensity, and the features of the entity that can cause harm justify the sense of the entity as dangerous. An emotion is inappropriate when our grasp of the underlying non-axiological features of the entity is incorrect or when the emotion is either not psychologically well motivated—something that is often noted by a second, negative self-assessing emotion—or not epistemically justified—something revealed by further examination of the non-axiological features of the entity and their relation to the appropriate value-concept.

Similarly, in the practical sphere, practical correctness is evidently attained when the action undertaken is right. (I put aside here the question of whether the term »right« should be understood as deontic or aretaic, but see Drummond 2022, 135). An action is right when the evaluation of the ends at which the action is aimed correctly grasps them as good, and when the evaluation of the specific character of the action as good is correct, and the action realizes its end. The performance of the positively valued action and the achievement of its positively valued end is the fulfillment of the practical intention (Drummond 2010, 449–56). It is important to note that the end might be internal or external to the action itself. If, for example, the end is external, as in building a storage shed, the end is realized only to the extent that the storage shed produced does the job well enough. If the shed falls over, the practical intention to build a storage shed is not fulfilled. By contrast and more important, if the end is internal and my aim, say, is to be honest, the end of being honest is realized in the very act of truth-telling itself.

In general, then, epistemic norms are essentially rooted in our nature as experiencing and rational agents. These norms are invariant across instances of the same experiential type. The epistemic norms are normative *for me* and *for us* just insofar as I and we are rational agents. Note, however, that these norms are largely content-neutral. A particular movement of the eyes will generate a flow of appearances manifesting particular phenomenal changes, but what those changes are will depend upon the seen thing and the same flow of appearances could be generated by keeping the eyes still and moving the head. Logical laws apply to terms and propositions in general; as formal, they are content-neutral. Similarly, in the brief discussion of emotions and volitions, we have identified normative structures rather than any content-full norms.

3. Practical norms

The situation changes when we turn to practical norms. The practical norms mentioned at the beginning are all rich in content. They have to do with the particular locations at which different kinds of eating utensils are to be placed, or they have to with instructions for how to carry out particular tasks or fill certain roles—for example, exactly where and roughly when the President, and only the President, shall appear before Congress to deliver the State of the Union Address, or they have to do with our expectations that people will behave in customary ways in particular social settings.

Since the discussions in the papers making up this volume are linked to ethics, I shall focus not on the previous examples but rather on examples that are tied to the kinds of overarching goods that Husserl calls »vocational goods« (Husserl 1989a, 28) or Charles Taylor calls »hypergoods« (Taylor 1989, 62–63) or Christine Korsgaard, from another perspective, calls »practical identities« (Korsgaard 1996, 101). These are goods—or identities—that give order, structure, and moral significance to a person's life-pursuits.

We are faced with many choiceworthy goods, but not all of them can be pursued and realized in a single life. The inability to realize them all does not, however, arise solely from their quantity. Rather, we decide from among these goods in relation to our physiological constitution and our experiential history, including recognizing the goods others in our family, our circle of acquaintances, and the larger society have chosen to value. More important, we decide among these goods in relation to our own capacities, talents, interests, concerns, and desires. Agents choose from among the available goods some subset of goods that are more or most highly valued in relation to these subjective factors. To identify a vocational good—whether being a spouse and parent, being a scientist or lawyer, engaging in politics, joining a religious community, attaining salvation, teaching and writing about philosophy, or, as in most, if not all, cases, some combination of such goods—is to identify the central goods to be pursued by us and to order other goods under them according to whether they are consistent with and more or less conducive to the overarching vocational goods. Vocational goods, which attract us as if »called« by them, are accompanied by a set of social rules and norms governing the activities and practices through which agents will realize them.

Imagine, for example, that I choose to be—among other important things such as a spouse, parent, and philosopher—a teacher. These four, partially overlapping »vocations« each aim at the goods proper to marriage, parenting, philosophizing, and teaching. In the case of teaching, that is to aim at the good of student learning. To be a teacher, then, is to do what teachers do in conducing to student learning. This entails adopting the norms governing the practices associated with being a teacher. These norms, as is the case with other practical norms, are conventional, formed over time, and handed down in the form of tradition. They can be passively accepted by someone who chooses to be a teacher, someone who does »what one does« as a teacher. Or they can be actively reflected upon in order to discern evidentially what should be preserved, what might be added, what might be adapted to one's own circumstances without fundamentally changing the norms, what might be modified in the norms, and, finally, what should be rejected. Think, for example, of the recent past in which teachers at all levels were faced with the immediate task of coming up with a revised set of practices and norms to govern teaching online or in hybrid situations in response to the COVID-19 pandemic.

Here the discussion of practical norms connects to the discussion of epistemic norms, and here we must prepare the ground for the distinction between first-order and second-order goods. The rational agent, we have said, seeks evidence in the various domains of reason, and in these evidential experiences »decides« for herself what is true and what false, what is valuable and what disvaluable, which actions are right and which wrong. This applies as well to her reflection on traditional norms; the rational agent reflects on these inheritances in the light of her evidential experiences. The contrast is with the agent who merely accepts passively the inherited norms or who, not committed to confirming her assumptions about teaching, judges without evidence; in either case, the agent merely supposes that the norms are valid. The agent does not »decide« for herself.

We must take care, however, when speaking of a »decision« about what is true, valuable, or right. It should not suggest some kind of subjectivism, some kind of constructivism, or some kind of voluntarism. The agent »decides« *in the light of evidential insight* whether to *appropriate*—to *take over* as her own—certain beliefs, attitudes, and practices. I am not denying freedom in matters of cognition, feeling, or acting. Our judgments are not caused by the things whose proper sense we seek, but they are (epistemically) normed both by what the things truly are and, as we have seen, by what we are—our experiential history, interests, concerns, and commitments to vocational goods. Our judgments are normed, in other words, by epistemic norms. It is truthfulness—cognitive, affective, and practical—not choice, that is fundamental to whether and how we appropriate norms.

The rational agent is a self-responsible agent, one who seeks evidence for her views, and upon gaining it, takes ownership of her beliefs, attitudes, and practices. She is autonomous insofar as she reflectively and consciously appropriates as her own conviction what is evidently experienced. Such a conviction—what Husserl calls a »habituality« (Husserl 1970a, 66)—becomes an enduring part of that subject's experiential life, one to which the subject can and does return again and again. The more continuous and consistent the confirmation is (or the agent takes it to be), the more the conviction determines future experience. It takes on the character of an »abiding habitus« that is dispositional in character (Husserl 1970a, 67), and this accounts for the fact that the agent in the course of future experiences takes certain features of the entity as salient relative to the previously adopted convictions informing the present experience.

The self-responsible agent in this way thinks for herself but not by herself. Truth is inherently and necessarily intersubjective, and to secure a conviction an agent must be aware that there exist possible defeaters and engage the views of others. The rational agent continually and reciprocally reflects on the truth and falsity of her convictions in concert with others. Her development is shaped by the influence of others—their thoughts, their feelings, and what they tell her about what one should and should not do. What is communicated influences her understanding of entities, of herself, and of social practices. In different circumstances and at different times, the effect on her development will be greater or lesser. An idea might influence her but not others—or vice versa—even though she and the others are in comparable circumstances. At the same time original thoughts arise in her or are originally inferred by her from her own beliefs, beliefs communicated to her, or traditional beliefs she has inherited.

The same is true of feelings: some arise originally in the agent, and some are acquired by a kind of contagion and felt only inauthentically. The thoughts, feelings, and instructions that come from others feel imposed, and this is often true of our first encounter with norms. More generally, we feel the impositions of morality, of custom, of tradition, and of the cultural milieu. An agent might yield to all these passively, even reluctantly. But an agent can also actively take a stand and freely appropriate, revise, or reject them on her own accord; the resultant beliefs thereby become her own. The agent's freedom, in other words, consists in the fact that she does not yield passively to the influence of others but »decides« for herself. This is the process through which practical norms, which are social constructs, come to be socially revised and in which we see how the development of a person and her identities is tethered to a cultural inheritance transmitted to us through the communicative medium of other individuals and traditions (Husserl 1989b, 281–82; see also 1970b, 353–78).

Tradition's transmission across generations calls attention to the historicality proper to both an individual's and a community's experience. A tradition, in brief, is a complex form of communal intentionality. Tradition shapes an individual's openness to the future in the light of the community's past. Traditions account for our initial understanding of empirical concepts, emotion concepts, value concepts, moral concepts, as well as the norms governing the practices associated with different vocations. It is against the background of this traditional understanding that, in becoming fully rational, we critically weigh the »proposals« before us and appropriate or modify or reject them. To put the matter another way, Stueber's second-order dispositions to consider the appropriateness of one's behavior are themselves rooted in epistemic norms and the teleological drive toward evidence.

To summarize, one becomes self-responsible in the transition from passively accepting beliefs handed down in tradition or proposed by others to the appropriation of a judgmental content as one's own conviction, one which has been tested against the convictions of others and for which one has intuitive evidence. Both the presentation of possibilities for one's life and the choice of a vocation arise for a subject by virtue of the social structure of intentionality, and the norms embedded in the agent's chosen vocation are binding precisely because the self-responsible person has secured for herself evidence for the cognitive and evaluative beliefs proper to this vocation as well as the rightness of the practices in and through which the vocational goods are realized. The full exercise of reason, in brief, entails both evidential truthfulness and self-responsibility; to exercise reason fully is to be a truthful agent responsible for what one believes, for one's evaluative attitudes toward things, and for what one does, including responsibility for one's overarching commitments, one's vocation. To be fully rational, in short, is to be, in an evidenced way, responsible for who one is.

Embedded in this account of evidence and self-responsibility is an ambiguity and a bifurcation in the notion of the good that points to the primacy of epistemic norms. Agents pursue goods, including vocational goods, as the object of first-order, contingent desires—what I call goods *for* an agent—as well as the second-order goods proper to self-responsible agency—what can be called the goods *of* agency (Drummond 2010, 420). The goods of agency are realized in an agent's making sense of the world as she becomes a self-responsible, truthful agent pursuing first-order goods (for herself and others). The goods of agency are superveniently and necessarily realized in first-order pursuits when those pursuits are evidentially realized. First-order goods for an agent are both necessarily transformed by and yield to the second-order goods of agency. If one is to be self-responsible, a chosen action as conducive to a first-order good for oneself or others must not frustrate (or frustrate least) the realization of necessarily valued second-order goods of agency for oneself or for others whose flourishing as rational agents is intertwined with my own.

We can now see both how socially constructed norms arise and become modified over time and what makes the norms governing the practices proper to an agent's vocation binding upon the agent. To put the matter another way, the demand for self-responsibility is grounded in the truth-interest proper to intentionality itself, an interest that establishes the governing norm for all human activity, namely, truthfulness (Drummond 2010; 2013; 2017). What accounts for the normativity of one's beliefs, feelings and attitudes, actions and practices is one's self-responsibly appropriating them on the basis of evidenced cognitions, emotions, and choices. The normativity of our everyday norms is grounded in our self-responsible convictions about the efficacy of those norms in truthfully shaping the beliefs, attitudes, and practices proper to our social and vocational lives.

A possible objection to this view is that the choice of—the commitment to—vocational goods is not itself intentional since it cannot be fulfilled in the manner proper to intentionality. The choice of a vocation, the objection goes, conditions how objects show up for us insofar as the choice of the vocation determines what features of things are salient to the agent pursuing the chosen vocation. The vocational choice, therefore, is pre-intentional. The vocational choice, in other words, is a condition, not an instance, of intentionality and the meaningfulness of things.

In response, I offer two points. First, recall the previous point about how the possibilities for vocational choice have been presented in our social interactions and historical traditions, in both of which intentional relations are clearly involved. Second, I want to consider a particular kind of choice that is involved in vocational choices and that I call »resolve.« Having self-responsibly appropriated certain beliefs, values, and norms relevant for different vocations, which, by the way, is a continuing and continual process, I resolve to realize the goods entailed by my chosen vocation and to perform those actions that conduce to those goods. Resolve presupposes the reflection on goods and the identification of superordinate goods. Resolve is the choice to advance those goods—say, the goods proper to teaching—by choosing to do what will realize those goods. The norms embedded in a chosen vocation are self-responsibly binding on an agent precisely because (1) the agent has secured evidence for (a) the cognitive and evaluative beliefs proper to this vocation as well as (b) the rightness of the practices in and through which the vocational goods are realized and because (2) the agent has resolved to realize those goods.

Resolve is a special kind of choice because it falls between what Husserl calls *Handlungswille,* an action-will (or, in John Searle's and John McDowell's terms, an intention-in-action), and an *Entschlußwille,* a decision-will, a decision to act in the future. Resolve is like *Entschlußwille* insofar as it involves an intention prior to action. The end in resolve is internal to the activity attempting to realize the resolution. I resolve to be a teacher, and I *am* a teacher when I *do* what teachers do. As John McDowell notes, a future intention—a decision-will—becomes an intention-in-action once the actions fulfilling the intention commence. Intending to make an omelet, I break the eggs, heat and grease the skillet, add the eggs and other ingredients, and voilà, there's the omelet and the action is completed; the intention is fully realized. At each moment of that process, however, the intention-in-action maintains itself both as an empty intention, not yet fulfilled, and, at the very same moment, as partially fulfilled. In the case of resolving to be a teacher, however, the intention-in-action is never to be fully realized; it is always in a state of partial completion, and adjustments in the actions undertaken to realize the ends of teaching are always available to me in the light of reflection on what I am doing and on how best to achieve the end of student learning. The actions that fulfill my resolve to be a teacher comprise an indefinite number of actions that are executed over a time of indefinite duration. In doing what teachers do, I not only *am* a teacher; I continuously resolve to be a teacher. This too manifests an intentional structure. Given these kinds of considerations, I suggest, committing oneself to a practical identity and its vocational goods is neither pre-intentional nor pre-rational nor lacking fulfillment, although it has its own proper mode of (partial) fulfillment.

It is my resolving to be something that makes practical norms normative for me. It is the epistemic norms proper to all the domains of reason—cognitive-theoretical, axiological, and practical—that ensure the choiceworthiness of the goods I pursue and provide the basis for properly identifying the practical norms that serve the ends set by my resolve. If a set of practical norms is irrelevant to the vocations central to my life, I will not feel them as binding just because they do not enter into my resolution to achieve vocational goods. I might still conform to them for prudential reasons or in just lazily going along with what »one« does, but they are not felt as binding on me, as obligatory, in the way that the evidentially grasped norms conducing to my chosen practical identity are binding. This bindingness, however, is inseparable from my evidential grasp of the truthfulness of my beliefs, attitudes, and choices.

I can, it is true, choose to reject epistemic norms and to pay no attention to evidence. But it is impossible to make this choice and to be a rational agent. I can, however, reject particular practical social norms and still be rational. I would be acting rationally when I choose not to be bound by norms that commit me to ends that are not truly goods or when adhering to the rejected norms would not best conduce to the ends proper to my truthful vocational choices. Rationally evidencing the social, practical norms proper to my evidenced vocational choices just is to conform to the epistemic norms essential to rational agency. These epistemic norms in conjunction with resolve account for the normativity of practical norms for me.

References

Bicchieri, Cristina, Ryan Muldoon, and Alessandro Sontuoso. 2018. Social Norms. In *The Stanford Encyclopedia of Philosophy*, edited by Edward N. Zalta, Winter 2018. Metaphysics Research Lab, Stanford University. https://plato.stanford.edu/archives/win2018/entries/social-norms/.

Crane, Tim. 2001. Intentional Objects. *Ratio* 14 (4): 336–49.

Drummond, John J. 1979. On Seeing a Material Thing in Space: The Role of Kinaesthesis in Visual Perception. *Philosophy and Phenomenological Research* 40 (1): 19–32.

—. 2010. Self-Responsibility and Eudaimonia. In *Philosophy Phenomenology Sciences*, edited by Carlo Ierna, Hanne Jacobs, and Filip Mattens, 441–60. Dordrecht: Springer.

—. 2012. Intentionality without Representationalism. In *The Oxford Handbook of Contemporary Phenomenology*, edited by Dan Zahavi, 115–33. Oxford: Oxford University Press.

—. 2013. Phenomenology, Eudaimonia, and the Virtues. In *Phenomenology and Virtue Ethics*, ed by Kevin Hermberg and Paul Gyllenhammer, 97–112. New York: Bloomsbury Academic.

—. 2017. Having the Right Attitudes. *The New Yearbook for Phenomenology and Phenomenological Philosophy* 15: 142–63.

—. 2022 Sympathetic Respect, Respectful Sympathy. *Ethical Theory and Moral Practice* 25 (1): 123–137.

Husserl, Edmund. 1969. *Formal and Transcendental Logic*. Translated by Dorion Cairns. The Hague: Martinus Nijhoff.

—. 1970a. *Cartesian Meditations: An Introduction to Phenomenology*. Translated by Dorion Cairns. The Hague: Martinus Nijhoff.
—. 1970b. *The Crisis of European Sciences and Transcendental Phenomenology: An Introduction to Phenomenological Philosophy*. Translated by David Carr. Evanston, IL: Northwestern University Press.
—. 1973. *Experience and Judgment: Investigations in a Genealogy of Logic*. Edited by Ludwig Landgrebe. Translated by James S. Churchill and Karl Ameriks. Evanston, IL: Northwestern University Press.
—. 1989a. *Aufsätze und Vorträge (1922–1937)*. Edited by Thomas Nenon and Hans Rainer Sepp. The Hague: Martinus Nijhoff.
—. 1989b. *Ideas Pertaining to a Pure Phenomenology and to a Phenomenological Philosophy. Second Book: Studies in the Phenomenology of Constitution*. Translated by Richard Rojcewicz and André Schuwer. Dordrecht: Kluwer.
—. 1997. *Thing and Space: Lectures of 1907*. Translated by Richard Rojcewicz. Dordrecht: Kluwer Academic Publishers.
—. 2001a. *Analyses Concerning Passive and Active Synthesis: Lectures on Transcendental Logic*. Translated by Anthony Steinbock. Dordrecht: Kluwer.
—. 2001b. *Logical Investigations*. Edited by Dermot Moran. Translated by J. N. Findlay. Vol. 2. 2 vols. London and New York: Routledge.
—. 2014. *Ideas for a Pure Phenomenology and Phenomenological Philosophy. First Book: General Introduction to Pure Phenomenology*. Translated by Daniel O. Dahlstrom. Indianapolis, IN: Hackett Publishing Company.
Korsgaard, Christine M. 1996. *The Sources of Normativity*. Cambridge and New York: Cambridge University Press.
Stueber, Karsten R. 2005. How to Think about Rules and Rule Following. *Philosophy of the Social Sciences* 35 (3): 307–23.
Taylor, Charles. 1989. *Sources of the Self: The Making of the Modern Identity*. Cambridge, MA: Harvard University Press.

Alessio Rotundo

The Ethnologist's Judgment: Raymond Aron and Maurice Merleau-Ponty on Interpreting Culture

Part One. Raymond Aron and the Ethnologist's Judgment

In his UNESCO text entitled *Race and History* (1952), Lévi-Strauss stated that »[t]he barbarian is first of all the man who believes in barbarism« (Lévi-Strauss 1983 [1952], 330).[1] This statement is presented in the context of a critique of the modern concept of humanism, and its universalistic demands, especially when this entails a principle of discrimination and subordination of those (in this case the »primitive«) who do not share the universalistic aspirations of our own civilization. For Lévi-Strauss, this principle of discrimination, however, only highlights the conformity of »civilized« thought to the logic underlying so-called »primitive« people, which is defined precisely as a logic of discrimination between »us« (the members of the tribe, as »good«, »complete«, etc.) and »them« (those excluded from participatory privileges within the circle of the tribe, who therefore are deemed »evil« or »incomplete«) (ibid.). In this way, our modern civilization and its »humanism« is realigned with every other humanity in history. As a result, we, and every other humanity of the present and of the past, are all barbarians because we all, in some way or other, believe in barbarism. Thus, for Lévi-Strauss, the supposed humanism of global civilized society does not escape the paradox of cultural relativism.

The rejection of the idea of a hierarchy of cultures in anthropology leads to a reassessment of the meaning of historical humanity

[1] The references to the works of Lévi-Strauss and Merleau-Ponty in this essay are to the available English translation with the original year of publication in square brackets. The translations from Aron's works are all mine. References to Aron's texts are to the available French editions followed by original publication year in square brackets.

that aims at dissolving not the difference among cultures, whose nature ethnology attempts to appreciate and clarify, but the very possibility of evolutionary and philosophical anthropology. This idea is also at the center of the thesis in *La pensée sauvage* (1962) about the basic commonality of thinking structures between primitive and modern societies: »It means still remaining faithful to the inspiration of wild thought to recognize that the scientific mind, in its most modern form, will have contributed, through an encounter that it alone could have predicted, to legitimizing the principles of wild thought and reestablishing its rights« (Lévi-Strauss 2021 [1962], 306–307). Far from simply rejecting this relativistic interpretation of culture, in his article on Lévi-Strauss from 1970, Raymond Aron points out the moral ambiguity affecting this critique of humanism, which has ultimately to do with an insufficient elaboration of the limits of cultural relativism. Aron points out that once every distinction between the primitive mind, which refuses to attribute full humanity to others, and the civilized mind, which aspires to attribute humanity to every human being, has been rejected, it becomes logically impossible to critique the racists, whose thinking again simply responds to the »barbarian« logic shared by both primitive and civilized people. The alternative to this impasse, following Aron, would be to affirm the »moral superiority« of that human society that, while often falling short of its own demands, recognizes the participation of all human beings in the idea of humanity (Aron 1970, 944). But this is precisely what Lévi-Strauss refuses to do, since this would imply the ratification of a historical and moral progress leading up to such recognition, thereby establishing, as a matter of fact, a hierarchy of cultures.

Lévi-Strauss wants to make a judgment about the equality of different cultures while refusing to elaborate the moral as well as epistemological implications of this same judgment in the context of his anthropology, which he nonetheless claims to be a rigorously scientific endeavor. The result is the paradox affecting any form of cultural relativism that does not critically reflect upon and makes explicit the scope and limits of relativistic interpretations. In the same vein, the ethnologist Lévi-Strauss universalizes cultural relativism while refusing to evaluate his own judgment about the »barbarism« of cultures. Aron's analysis suggests a correction of both the common interpretation of cultural relativism and the mistaken interpretations positing our civilization as absolute paradigm of evaluation of civilization as such. The universal claim of relativism remains tied to a perspective that the interpreter chooses. Lévi-Strauss posits the equality among cultures by universalizing »barbarism« in such a way that, if taken literally, would devoid his own anthropological enterprise of all meaning. If cultures are equal in their »barbarism«, why can only the ethnologist Lévi-Strauss understand them?

Aron's response to the impasse of cultural relativism is articulated in two main moments that should be read as working together. The first thing to notice is that the recognition of the humanity of all human beings is essentially related to the recognition that there are no values, determinations, and truths that are independent from a system of reference. In this sense, a relativistic interpretation of culture seems inevitable if this is simply taken to mean that there is no »view from nowhere« and that the historian, the ethnologist, and even the philosopher are never in possession of a definitive interpretation of the fate of humanity or a universal system of values which would hold good for everyone. The recognition of a multiplicity of perspectives, however, does not have to issue into the absolute idiosyncrasy of an unqualified relativistic »barbarism« defining every human culture. This idiosyncrasy seems to have to follow from the impossibility to establish a univocal and positive system of reference for evaluating all cultures.[2] But the impossibility to evaluate manifold cultural expressions with reference to one common and overarching standard does not *ipso facto* entail incommunicability and cultural isolation. This traditional version of relativism is intrinsically paradoxical, since it only shifts the absolute standard of evaluation into each cultural system taken as measure of itself and therefore as ultimately incomparable with any other. The result is the perfect equivalence of all cultures. On the contrary, this paradoxical form of absolute relativism is overcome in the very moment in which one recognizes the partiality of one's own perspective, which enables the recognition of the plurality of other perspectives and thus of their potential reciprocal communication (cf. Aron 2011 [1946], 40). Rather than being a negation of relation to others, this latter form of relativism precisely affirms that no cultural system simply rests on itself as having only

2 This »unique sense« of human existence, »normative for all«, Aron writes in an article on *La philosophie de l'histoire,* as such »has never existed either on earth or in heaven.« Aron 2011 [1946], 40.

in itself its own absolute criterion of truth. If the recognition of the humanity of all human beings therefore requires the recognition of the plurality of human experience, we now see that the recognition of these different experiences as human requires the recognition of a common human condition: »the recognition of humanity in every human being (or, if one prefers, of the human species) has the recognition of human plurality as a condition or as an immediate consequence. The human being is the being that speaks but there are thousands of different languages. Whoever forgets one of these two terms relapses into barbarism« (Aron 1970, 950). Lévi-Strauss' refusal to recognize the progress towards the awareness of a common participation of all human beings in the same human condition is thus based on the assumption that communication and exchange would only be possible on the basis of a positive and common human standard, which for him the modern civilizations and especially *our* civilization erroneously believe to represent, in spite of their evident »equivocations and regressions.«

The succession of cultures appears in this context like a discontinuous series rather than a development. This conclusion is in line with the critique of the diachronic model of history as »more specific human order« and, more specifically, of evolutionary theories in the tradition of social anthropology.[3] At the same time, this view is critical of those attempts aimed at apprehending *historical unity* and a possible *determination of the sense* of human history. But Lévi-Strauss' critique of the »special prestige« assigned to continuity and unity in history is functional for raising a critique against the ethnocentrism of modern humanism stemming from the alleged ontological primacy

[3] »The ethnologist respects history, but does not give it a privileged status. He conceives of it as a form of research complementary to his own: one unfolds the range of human societies in time, the other in space [...] This symmetrical relation between history and ethnology seems to be rejected by philosophers who, implicitly or explicitly, contest the idea that distribution in space and succession in time offer equivalent perspectives. It might be said that in their eyes, the temporal dimension enjoys special prestige, as though diachrony founded a type of intelligibility not only superior to that offered by synchrony, but above all of a more specifically human order. It is easy to explain (if not to justify) this opinion: the diversity of social forms that ethnology grasps in their distribution in space appears as a discontinuous system: and it is supposed that, thanks to the temporal dimension, history restores to us, not separate states, but the passage from one state to another in a continuous form.« Lévi-Strauss 2021 [1962], 291–292. Cf. on this point, Goldman 2004, 100–102.

of a particular view of humanity at the expense again of sociocultural differences and alterity.[4]

The cultural relativism of the ethnologist must issue in an especially paroxysmal form of historical relativism. With this result, we can now highlight the second main point of Aron's response, which pivots around the elaboration of the limits of relativism. The principal point of this response can be summarized as follows. The awareness that one's perspective is oriented by a direction of interest that is necessarily selective, since it determines the system of reference for one's value-judgments, does not issue into the hopeless paradoxes of a skeptical relativism and in the rejection of the philosophy of history. This conclusion is based on two interrelated sets of considerations that Aron elaborates in various texts on the theme of history.

1) The first set of considerations takes up the problem of a universal human society in relation with the development of science, in particular the development of modern positive science, based on the notions of causality, quantification, experiment, verification and falsification. In this connection Aron asks the following question: »All languages, all cultures are human, they express *one* humanity. But does not the language of science have legitimately a privilege insofar as in taking up all languages as its object and in being virtually available to everyone, it alone founds the humanity of all human beings by the potential universality of truth?« (Aron 1970, 950). In an article published for the *Bulletin of the Atomic Scientists* in 1964, Aron

[4] Lévi-Strauss attributes the »prejudice« of continuity to a particular belief of our own culture, i.e. the »totalizing continuity of the *ego*«: »And since we ourselves believe that we apprehend our personal evolution as continuous change, historical knowledge seems to confirm the evidence of our inner sense.« See Lévi-Strauss 2021 [1962], 292. In a later interview from 1979, Lévi-Strauss will explicitly name Descartes, but also the Judeo-Christian tradition, and the humanism of the Renaissance as contributing to this ethnocentric conception. See Jacquet-Francillon 2017, 9. In a text from 1956 with the title »The Three Humanisms«, included in the second volume of *Anthropologie structurale*, Lévi-Strauss had already outlined a version of this criticism in his distinction of three kinds of humanism: the »aristocratic« humanism of the Renaissance, which selected a restrictive version of the human being as model of the whole of humanity, and the »bourgeois« humanism of the nineteenth century, which remained attached to the commercial and colonial means of its encounter with other cultures, were both taken to be representatives of ethnocentric humanistic views. Lévi-Strauss rather proposed the »democratic« humanism of ethnology as being truly universal. See Lévi-Strauss 1983 [1956], 271–274.

already highlighted the moral scope of this question: »Here, indeed, is the core of the argument – is the rationality of modern societies more than a means? Does it imply – must it logically imply – the application of moral principles to societies, a trend toward respect for humanitarian values?« (Aron 1964, 23). While Aron denies that a »logical or scientific connection« would exist »between science and a scientific attitude in other fields«, he concludes that »[s]cientific rationality tends to set up the idea of a universal society of all mankind. The twentieth century ideal is loftier than that of any of the closed societies of the past, which countenanced moral barriers between races and between people« (ibid.). The idea of human unity is not new, but the expansion of industrial technologies and the material and economic homogenization of life through the rationalization of the means of production are on the way to actually realize a common human civilization based on the progressive accumulation of »knowledge and power.«[5] At the same time, Aron stresses the double aspect of the last century, »imbued by the intellectual, technical, and economic revolution that like a cosmic force sweeps humanity along towards an unknown future, but in certain respects it resembles many other centuries coming before it, since it is not the first century of great wars. On the one hand, the necessity of progress, on the other, *history as usual* and the drama of empires, armies, and heroes« (Aron 2011 [1960], 237). This double aspect is reflected in the contemporary awareness that while science and technology are uniting the whole of humanity, thereby suggesting the possibility of a history guided by the »accumulation towards a final term«, this is at the same time the awareness that no such process is guaranteed in advance (cf. Aron 2011 [1946], 50; 2011 [1959], 124). As a result, while the universalistic philosophies of history of the nineteenth century appear to be inadequate for achieving an understanding of our time, the reflection about the global expansion of scientific rationality, industry, and technical mastery of entire domains of our life can and must still raise the question about the »universal vocation« of human reason (Aron 2011 [1960], 255). In his 1960 Lord Samuel Lecture on »The Dawn of Universal History«, Aron thus concludes that »[n]othing proves that the times [of suffering and human blood] are over and that the rational process would extend without dramas. Maybe universal

5 See on this point Aron 2011 [1959], 125; 2011 [1960], 237, 245.

history is different than the provincial histories of past millennia. This is only a hope supported by faith« (Aron 2011 [1960], 254).

2) A second set of remarks coalesces at this juncture. The effort to determine a sense of human history that would at the same time respond to the demands of scientific rationality poses a problem to the methodology of the historian and his or her claims to historical objectivity. While »the limit between a *historical reconstruction*, which belongs to positive knowledge, and a *philosophy*, which surpasses this knowledge toward the myth, will always lack exactness«, at the end of his article Aron reproaches Lévi-Strauss for refusing to make explicit and define the relationship between the scientific task of historical reconstruction and the philosophy of history attaching more or less explicitly to every historical account. Aron reads this refusal on the part of Lévi-Strauss to answer the question about the relationship and difference between science, philosophy, and history as an implicit critique of the philosophy of history (Aron 1970, 951–952).[6] This linkage of historical meaning to scientific efforts of rational cognition is not a ratification of radical relativism but the open recognition of a transcendental condition for rational objectivity, namely that the actualization of rational cognition in some shareable meaning transcending cultural and social particularity is always actualization of a potentiality for validation or falsification within an intersubjective community in the complex medium of cultural institutions, social apparatuses, and this governed by the basic determinant of language. If a final coincidence between scientific reconstruction, which must always work within the limitations of historical and social determinants, and the determination of a meaning in history must remain ultimately elusive, this only demonstrates that no cultural entity can claim historical finality, which therefore ought to sanction the »final uncertainty of our historical consciousness« as ongoingly dynamic and essentially unfinished.[7] One could certainly link this uncertainty to our historicism, which Aron in his article on *La philosophie de l'his-*

6 Cf. the following statement on this very point from an earlier essay: »A historian does not always have, as such, a philosophy of history, elaborated in full detail. He can or even must, perhaps, demarcate the limits of our knowledge, the unpredictability of the future, the mystery of supposed laws, but, explicitly or not, he makes for himself a certain idea of the schemas of the becoming and meaning of the historical reality for the human being.« Aron 2011 [1959], 107.

7 On the relationship between the scientific task of historiography and the interpretation of the meaning of history, see Aron 2011 [1959], 109; cf. 2011 [1946], 41. On

toire, with reference to Meinecke, defines as »the attentive consciousness of the lived experiences and works made by man in the course of the centuries in their inexhaustible wealth« (Aron 2011 [1946], 47; cf. Aron 2011 [1959], 121). Historical consciousness, however, is not only consciousness of plurality but, as *consciousness*, also apprehends the plurality of human experiences as the very expression of human life rather than as evidence of an insurmountable contradiction. This historical awareness resolves the »barbaric« conflict of cultures by elevating the discontinuity of the manifold of dogmatic perspectives into the dimension of historical continuity.[8]

According to this concept of historical consciousness, progress towards the universalism of human society must not entail absolutism of values and it is compatible with an irreducible plurality of patterns of existence. Aron states that the historical consciousness of modern Europe is the truly defining idea taking hold of humanity as a whole, even more so than the unification of a global humanity engaging in the same scientific and technological endeavors (Aron 2011 [1959], 106). This is a point that Aron stresses repeatedly across his writings on history. His essay entitled *De l'objet de l'histoire* opens and closes with this very point:

> The success of the philosophy of history, in spite of the progress of historical science, can therefore be easily explained by the refusal to ignore the sense (direction and meaning) of a becoming that touches the very substance of humanity. The knowledge of the past enthralls the human being, he is not satisfied by the results of science because the succession of societies captivates his very soul (Aron 2011 [1959], 107).

> Historical situation or human condition: historical knowledge does not and cannot ignore either of these two terms because human beings today must interrogate the scope of the revolution that they are undergoing and the sense that, beyond knowledge and the machines, they want to give to their existence (Aron 2011 [1959], 126).

---

the notion of historical consciousness as »uncertain« or unfinished, see Aron 2011 [1959], 125.

[8] »Historical relativism is so to speak surpassed as soon as the historian stops aiming at an impossible detachment, recognizes his point of view and, as a result, puts himself in the condition to recognize the perspectives of others. This does not mean that one could, strictly speaking, go from one perspective to another: there is no numerical constant or calculable equivalence. But one comes to understand the perspectives, even when they appear contradictory, and to see in their multiplicity an expression of life and not the sign of a loss.« Aron 1946 [2011], 40. Cf. Aron 2011 [1959], 123.

But it would be a mistake to identify this sense, direction, and meaning – i.e. the presence of *Reason* in history – with any particular expression of culture or society, as Aron concludes in his essay entitled *La notion du sens de l'histoire*:

> [I]t is as much a mistake to give to oneself in thinking a social state in which all the aspirations would be fulfilled at once, as much as it is legitimate to construe an idea of reason, the representation of an orderly and equitable collectivity that would retrospectively appear as the *raison d'être* of the long painful and bloody path of humanity […] But to confuse this idea of Reason with the action of a party, with regulations of property, with a technique of economic organization is to deliver oneself to the madness of fanaticism. Wanting history to have a sense is inviting the human being to master his nature and make the life in common conform to reason. Assuming to know in advance the final sense and the ways of salvation is to substitute historical mythologies to the ungrateful progress of knowledge and action (Aron 2011 [1957], 65).

But already in 1946, Aron would conclude his reflection on »The Philosophy of History« with the statement that »[t]he absence and the need of a philosophy of history are thus equally characteristic of our time. Humanity is aware to be engaging in an adventure in which both its soul and its existence are at stake. It would no longer abandon itself to the illusory gods of progress and history. What nourishes its yearning is not the regret for convenient schemes, which have been cleared away by the success of erudition. Humanity accepts a patient and lengthy exploration that is by nature unfinished« (Aron 2011 [1946], 51).

From this critical understanding of historical consciousness there emerges the conception of a »pluralist anthropology« that Aron already presented in his doctoral thesis on the philosophy of history and the objectivity of historical knowledge. The overarching point of Aron's early work can be perhaps best grasped if we link the opening statements to the ones that close his study. These statements pivot around the thesis that any retrospective knowledge marks a gap between the lived experience of individuals and collectivities and the posthumous reconstruction of historical sense: »All the analyses that follow are dominated by this claim that man is not only in history, but that he carries in himself the history that he explores« (Aron 1948 [1938], 11). Historical knowledge is and can only be effective within the very historical structure of human life. The retrospective efforts of historical knowledge display therefore an »original solidarity of subject and object«, which must marshal the methodological and ontological aspects of a theory of history beyond the limiting dualisms of the tradition (Aron 1948 [1938], 53, 56). The conception of a pluralist anthropology opposes dogmatic forms of historical determinism that either dissolve historical unity into a chain of self-enclosed atomic units (Spengler) or subject each atomic unit to the overarching power of anonymous forces, whether psychological or sociological, that are completely separated from conscious human action while at the same time leading humanity to its vocational realization (Marx). The problem of determinism in history, as conceptual translation of a regular succession of events, becomes genuine interrogation of history if it is not opposed to the advent of contingency and rather recuperates history at the point in which individuals or the whole of humanity begin to reflect about their contingency and situation:

> Again we arrive at plurality, plurality of spiritual universes, of ideal forces as well as of real forces. Dialectical plurality, as it were: a kind of solidarity is established between the situations and human volitions, between reality and idea, which is not to be assimilated to a raw determinism or to a sterile reproduction, but to the creative reaction of a conscious being (Aron 1948 [1938], 277).

This conception of a pluralist anthropology implies and exhibits the human being as a »dialectic of existence.« This dialectic on the one hand excludes eternal and transcendent reason: »There is nothing on this side of or beyond becoming: humanity is confounded with its history, the individual with its duration« (Aron 1948 [1938], 345). On the other hand, the same dialectic makes room for the pursuit of reason: »[This is] no doubt a historical dialectic, but constantly determined to overcome history and defined by this will, which is always in vain and always resumed. Because history would disappear if the human being had nothing more to learn but also if he would never learn anything« (Aron 1948 [1938], 321). Even if in this limited way, Aron's theory of history offers a sober response to the impasse of relativism.

Part Two. Merleau-Ponty and Social Anthropology

The ambiguity of Lévi-Strauss' attribution of »barbarism« to the humanity that denies inhumanity stems from his rejection of the notion of a meaning in history and thus from a critique of the philosophy of history as the effort to establish a unitary sense and direction of human life. While this rejection is instrumental to Lévi-Strauss' critique of ethnocentrism, Aron has shown that the obliteration of the philosophy of history rests more fundamentally on an insufficient elaboration of a theory of history and of the notion of historical consciousness. In his text on the relationship between »History and Ethnology« from 1949, Lévi-Strauss argues for a complementary role of history and ethnology in the study of social life. But the role of history in the human sciences, while legitimate and even necessary, is subordinated to the task of singling out elementary structures that operate like anonymous mechanisms in the thinking and praxis of human beings:

> Thus, anthropology cannot remain indifferent to historical processes and to the most highly conscious expressions of social phenomena. But if the anthropologist brings to them the same scrupulous attention as the historian, it is in order to eliminate, by a kind of backward course, all that they owe to the historical process and to conscious thought. His goal is to grasp, beyond the conscious and always shifting images which men hold, the complete range of unconscious possibilities (Lévi-Strauss 1963 [1949], 23).

This programmatic statement will find an unequivocal and famous confirmation in the last chapter of *La pensée sauvage*: »The final goal of the human sciences is not to constitute man, but to dissolve [*dissoudre*] him« (Lévi-Strauss 2021 [1962], 281). It is in the context of this program that cultural relativism is raised by Lévi-Strauss to a foundational principle of social anthropology. As Aron indicates at the end of his essay on Lévi-Strauss, only the critical consideration of the epistemological and methodological sense of structural analysis can therefore deliver a substantive critique of the thesis of relativism that this analysis advances.[9] Now it is precisely around this point that Maurice Merleau-Ponty leverages his critique of relativism in anthropology. In his article on Lévi-Strauss, Merleau-Ponty lays out

[9] Cf. on this point Broekman 1971, 130.

the epistemological tenets of structural analysis in anthropology and concludes that far from simply establishing invariant and universal archetypes, the »most proper task of anthropology« is the »joining« of objective analysis and lived experience: »The variables of anthropology, on the contrary, must be met sooner or later on the level at which phenomena have an immediately human significance« (Merleau-Ponty 1964 [1959], 119). This linkage has of course to do with the fact that in phenomenology structures of intentional engagement are taken to be fundamental for the coalescing of any meaning. One thing to be noted therefore is that Merleau-Ponty interprets ethnological experience in conjunction with the critical recasting of the autonomy and freedom attributed to the constituting transcendental subjectivity in the tradition of idealistic philosophies, including certain preliminary presentations of phenomenology.

While the crucial matter of rethinking the theory of constitution in transcendental philosophy cannot be adequately represented here, let it suffice to note that Merleau-Ponty's theory of perceptual consciousness from his early studies grounds the idea of constituting consciousness squarely in the reflective act of the incarnated, individual, and historical subject that discovers and actualizes that very idea.[10] Once consciousness is recognized in its inherent individuality, then one must also recognize a constant *engagement from beyond* the reflective consciousness itself that is essential to the formation and determination of transcendental meaning as effectuated by reflective operations.[11] The necessity of this engagement as structural condition for thought is one of Merleau-Ponty's signature insights and one that he unshakably expands and deepens in his 1950s lecture courses. These courses systematically show how reflection already works and must continue to work from *within* a perceptual »field«, a linguistic »field«, a social »field«, a historical »field« as principal constitutive

10 This move is motivated by the nature of the constituting process as ultimately temporalizing. With the process of temporalization, however, phenomenology is confronted with a »givenness« that conditions and is therefore the very medium of accessibility for any experiential sense and reflective determination of this sense as transcendental. What this concretely implies is that ultimate constituting subjectivity as temporal cannot be accessed by way of the same experiential modalities to which it gives rise while being able to be recognized only in the very concrete experiential modalities that actually open our engagement in the world.

11 I take the expression »engagement from beyond« from an article by Ronald Bruzina on the theme of language in Husserlian phenomenology. See Bruzina 1981, 363.

conditions of experience that are essential to reflection if it has to have at all the radical role that Merleau-Ponty assigns to it as »construction« of a genesis of sense that it does not stop thinking and must in the end account for.[12]

It is this kind of thinking that Merleau-Ponty detects in ethnology as a form of »actual thinking« (*pensée effective*) that »moves back and forth between experience and intellectual construction and reconstruction« (Merleau-Ponty 1964 [1955], 119). If what characterizes ethnology is that it »takes man in his actual situation of life and understanding«, then the »structures« that the ethnologist posits as the logical principles and operations underlying human societies are the very principles and operations in which structuralist analysis remains itself inchoate as analysis that begins in the living situation of the anthropologist.[13] The method of ethnology thus actualizes »a

---

12 Merleau-Ponty describes the constitutive originality of the irreflective dimensions of our experience everywhere in his works. The »Preface« to the *Phenomenology of Perception* makes this point unequivocally and paradigmatically clear with the claim that »philosophy is an ever-renewed experiment of its own beginning, that it consists entirely in describing this beginning, and finally, that radical reflection is conscious of its own dependence on an unreflected life that is its initial, constant, and final situation.« See Merleau-Ponty 2012 [1945], lxxviii. This dependence on an unreflected life expresses the definitive inclusion of reflective consciousness in the »temporal flow« as »primordial fact« and »permanent situation« of any act of consciousness. See Merleau-Ponty 1973 [1955], 138n78. We find the same realization being forcefully articulated in the opening chapter of *Le visible et l'invisible* on »Reflection and Interrogation«, especially in the section entitled »The Perceptual Faith and Reflection.« Merleau-Ponty 1968 [1964], 28–49. On the concept of »construction« in phenomenology, see Bruzina 2001.

13 Cf. on this point Bimbenet 2004, 313. On the concept of »structure«, cf. Merleau-Ponty 1964 [1955], 117. In the essay entitled *La métaphysique dans l'homme* from 1947, and after his two great studies about living behavior and human perception, Merleau-Ponty was already in full possession of the far-reaching scope of the notion of structure for psychology and linguistics. In both disciplines, Merleau-Ponty writes, it is a matter of »wholes« »which are not the pure manifestations of a directive consciousness, which are not explicitly aware of their own principles, and which nevertheless can and should be studied by proceeding from the whole to the parts.« Merleau-Ponty 1964 [1947], 87–88. In the same essay, Merleau-Ponty turns to sociology to draw an analogous conclusion: each society appears to sociology as a »totality where phenomena give mutual expression to each other and reveal the same basic theme.« Merleau-Ponty 1964 [1947], 90. The modern efforts in the human sciences are here interpreted as sketching out a theory of the human spirit that recasts the separation of sensible matter and of cognitive a priori forms. The synthetic *a priori* judgments arising from this approach do not point to a constitutive ground where we find already actualized the conditions of possibility of knowledge, but

second way to the universal: no longer the overarching universal of a strictly objective method, but a sort of lateral universal which we acquire through ethnological experience and its incessant testing of the self through the other person and the other person through the self« (Merleau-Ponty 1964 [1959], 120).

The issue of cultural and historical relativity is therefore deeply transformed in the context of this conceptual framework. The import of this transformation can be best illustrated if we look at the other principal document of Merleau-Ponty's confrontation with Lévi-Strauss' anthropology. The lecture course that Merleau-Ponty held at the Collège de France in 1954–55 entitled *L'institution dans l'histoire personelle et publique* concludes with a critical analysis of the work of Lévi-Strauss and its thesis of relativism of cultures in connection with a reformulation of the task of the historian. Merleau-Ponty's thesis is straightforward: relativism is itself historical (Merleau-Ponty 2010 [2003], 64; cf. Merleau-Ponty 1964 [1955], 30–31, 56). As a result, relativism must itself be relativized. In other words, the thesis about the impossibility of the philosophy of history, of the understanding of oneself and of others as parts of a common historical dimension that admits of sense and direction, is still the philosophy of an absolute or universal onlooker: »The absolute opacity of history, like its absolute light, is still philosophy conceived as closed knowledge. The one who observes the opacity sets himself up outside of history,

---

to the limits of the objectivity, and thus of the universality, that a communication between spirits can aspire to as never fully secured against the perils of breakdown. This is also the only conceivable actuality of a science of the human spirit. For Kant, human reason demands completeness in the effort to clarify the conditions of both theoretical and moral experience. This means that reason demands both the systematic totality of cognitions and the determination of an absolute principle as ground of this system. If Kant therefore defines metaphysics in accordance with the idea of a system, Merleau-Ponty offers almost a direct reply to this conception when he writes: »metaphysics is the opposite of the system. If system is an arrangement of concepts which makes all the aspects of experience immediately compatible and compossible, then it suppresses metaphysical consciousness and, moreover, does away with morality at the same time.« Merleau-Ponty 1964 [1947], 94. For Merleau-Ponty, what is distinctive in the original notion of structure that social anthropology takes up and deepens in relation to human culture and history is the renewed attempt to name a type of being that calls into question »the classical alternative between ›existence as thing‹ and ›existence as consciousness‹«, and that rather puts the subjective and the objective in communication. See Merleau-Ponty 1964 [1947], 86. This is part of a pattern in the human sciences in which Merleau-Ponty recognizes a recast sense of metaphysics as a »metaphysics in the act.«

becomes a universal spectator« (Merleau-Ponty 2010 [2003], 63). The relativization of relativism as historical is not a reiteration of the paradox of absolute relativism and its thesis about the insularity of cultures and societies. One should note that this insularity contradicts the very idea of relativity since if one were to evaluate each culture only with respect to itself, then it would become impossible to detect cultural differences and thus to assert relativism.[14] When confronting a foreign culture, or even in front of the remains of a civilization that has disappeared, the »object« is recognized as a subjective expression that, in the absence of anything else, at the very least, is understood as *expression* or *symbol* of other human beings. But the domain in which this minimum understanding takes place, the dimension in which objects are recognized as being essentially related to a subjectivity for which they have or had a meaning, whose content we may obviously fail to grasp fully or at all, *is* history. In his Collège de France project proposal from 1951, Merleau-Ponty already indicated the trajectory of his reading of history as symbolism when he claimed that »[t]he idea of a single history or of a logic of history is, in a sense, implied in the least human exchange« and thus »anthropology supposes that civilizations very different from ours are comprehensible to us« (Merleau-Ponty 1964 [1951], 10). It should be noted that Merleau-Ponty's thesis of »historical symbolism« is also articulated in connection with the critical analysis of the Marxist philosophy of history that Merleau-Ponty developed around the same time of the study on institution. In a reading that freely draws from Marx's definition of capital, Merleau-Ponty writes:

> There are subjects, objects, there are men and things, but there is also a third order, that of relationships between men inscribed in tools or social symbols. These relationships have their development, their advances, and their regressions. Just as in the life of the individual, so in this generalized life there are tentative aims, failure or success, reaction of the result on the aim, repetition or variation, and this is what one calls history (Merleau-Ponty 1964 [1955], 38).

This passage makes clear that history is a »third order« in which antinomic terms are connected. In the lecture course on »Institution«,

---

[14] In his interpretive proposal of Lucien Febvre's study on *Le probléme de l'incroyance au XVI e siècle, la religion de Rabelais* (1942), Merleau-Ponty writes: »[idea of an] insularity of epochs. If they were insular, we would not even see their difference.« Merleau-Ponty 2010 [2003], 67.

this third order is clearly said to be transcendental.[15] This means that history is not on the same level of the particular cultures and civilizations that emerge, grow, and disappear but is rather the dimension of their compossibility within one same history. This reading of history outlines therefore a conception of historical understanding that directly challenges Lévi-Strauss' own reading of cultural difference in history: »modern man gave free rein to a hundred philosophical and sociological speculations in order to establish futile compromises between these contradictory poles and to account for the diversity of cultures, while seeking to suppress that which seems to him scandalous and shocking« (Lévi-Strauss 1983 [1952], 330). The attempt to reconcile the two contradictory poles of cultural difference and historical unity must remain futile so long as history is taken in conjunction with either of these disjunctive poles. But if history is more than just difference *or* unity, as being on a different plane than that of their antinomy, then the diversity of cultures, taken as incomparable units, is recomposed on another level than that in which difference is simply taken to be self-referential as having in itself its own criteria of evaluation and truth. If it is true, as Lévi-Strauss will write later, that »history is thus never history, but history-for« (Lévi-Strauss 2021 [1962], 293), this should not be understood as an *ontic* condition pertaining to different and incomparable perspectives but rather as the *transcendental* condition of their possible unity. Thus, a theory of history as »symbolism« has a double import. Firstly, it is a theory of historical understanding as a theory of the regulative use of the understanding that denies the idea of progress or evolution as absolute in relation to a fixed end of historical development, especially when this progress is taken to be coinciding with an arbitrary and particular entity within history. But secondly, it is a theory of historical understanding as critique of historical reason that connects different sociocultural realities in a common human horizon of communication and exchange.[16] While our experience must always be related to some

[15] »[…] history moreover which is not events, but right away intersubjectivity (transcendental history).« Merleau-Ponty 2010 [2003], 71.

[16] On Merleau-Ponty's trajectory for recasting a theory of reason, see the following programmatic passage from his article on Lévi-Strauss: »On a deeper level, anthropology's concern is neither to prove that the primitive is wrong nor to side with him against us, but to set itself up on a ground where we shall both be intelligible without any reduction or rash transposition. This is what we do when we take the symbolic function as the source of all reason and unreason. For the number and richness of

concrete cultural and historical setting, it is in principle open to other settings as in the very least *potentially* understandable – as ethnology also affirms and demonstrates by its concrete work. In discussing the problem of the communication between different historical periods at the end of the course on »Institution«, Merleau-Ponty aptly describes this basic sense of communication as »communication of an existential order« that is not »notional« (i.e. an order that must be based on available or positive cultural contents) and states that »in a sense, the first condition is to know also that they are not thoroughly *other*...« (Merleau-Ponty 2010 [2003], 108n35).

Now this sketch of a conception of history builds the premise for raising the question, which closes the whole lecture course, about the global interpretation of history and about the determination of a hierarchy of cultures:

> Problem: is there a field of world history or universal history? Is there an intended accomplishment? A closure on itself? A *true* society? The question is still, as in the history of knowledge, interrogation of history. But [what is at issue is an] existential, not conceptual, universal, which is inserted by this very interrogation. There is, if not true society (none of the existing societies is the true one, but even in principle no society can assert this), at least societies which ask themselves the question of the true society, »open societies« [...] [conceiving the] idea of a recuperation of history by means of history. And there are other societies that we can call relatively false in relation to those who pose the question of the true society. This does not mean that in certain relations they are not more beautiful. But they do not play the mysterious game which consists in putting all humans into the game, in attempting to make the intermingling truly universal. They follow the letter of institution but not its spirit, which consists in not being limited, prohibited, enclosed on an island of customs. The spirit of institution consists in setting an unlimited historical labor underway (Merleau-Ponty 2010 [2003], 72).

This text reasserts the idea that a universal history ending in some existing »true« society – a society that would be the truth of the whole of history – is inconceivable. Yet this conclusion does not

---

significations man has at his disposal always exceed the circle of definite objects which warrant the name ›signified‹, because the symbolic function must always be ahead of its object and finds reality only by anticipating it in imagination. Thus our task is to broaden our reasoning to make it capable of grasping what, in ourselves and in others, precedes and exceeds reason.« Merleau-Ponty 1964 [1955], 122.

yield an unqualified version of cultural or historical relativism. If the actualization of human understanding is always result of a work done within the strictures of cultural diversity and history, the reflective awareness that there is no last word about humanity and its history, i.e. *that* in historical existence there is always more to be done and said, and *that* anything that can be said and done about even a global human civilization never simply exhausts the potentiality of its history, also partially transcends the strictures of cultural and social particularity. Intersubjectivity across cultures and history is thus not only a limiting or finitizing factor for reflective and rational consciousness but the structural condition for its very realization, so that each aspect is necessary for an understanding of rationality and truth. Now for Merleau-Ponty it is precisely the openness to this kind of historical reason as inherently unfinished that should be interrogated as possible criterion for determining the sense of history and for interpreting culture. Lévi-Strauss admits that from the point of view of a particular cultural perspective there can be »accumulation« and progress, even if seen from the outside a certain culture may appear to be »stationary.« Thus, once »criteria« have been determined – that consists in »value judgments, motivations and centers of interest« (Lévi-Strauss 1983 [1952], 340) – a direction of development can also be reflected upon and evaluated. But if the separation between cultures is not absolute, if cultures are not absolutely incomparable, then the question about a progression of history as »cumulative« for the whole of humanity, as global interpretation of history, is not only legitimate but essential to humanity, assumed that the criteria for interpreting culture are themselves taken to be engaged in a living history that tests their validity and leaves open the possibility of »adventures, ruptures, and scandals« (Lévi-Strauss 1983 [1952], 361).[17]

[17] In the lecture course on »Institution«, this sketch of a conception of history is probed in systematic analyses of detail while also undergoing a generalization – which is said to have »metaphysical« scope – by a critical elaboration of the Husserlian notion of *Stiftung* or »institution.« This elaboration extracts from the notion of institution as both *instituting* and *instituted* the double thematic of history as rupture that inaugurates a new continuity and history as renewal that develops previous patterns. The two terms are never exclusive and build rather an antinomy that invites us to conceive a dimension where the poles of constancy of the instituted and the mutation initiated by the instituting event can be thought together without contradiction. This is a complex topic that Roberto Terzi analyzes extensively in his essay (2017). »La raison majeure d'intérêt du concept d'institution tient en effet à ceci, qu'il joint en lui, de façon synthétique, originaire et concrète, deux thèmes théoriques essentiels: 1) *la référence*

I will close this essay by tying up a loose end and opening another. Firstly, let me tie up the loose end. What is significant about Merleau-Ponty's critique of anthropological relativism is that it perfectly rejoins Aron's criticism of Lévi-Strauss by making explicit the main epistemological import of structural analysis, which was Aron's main complaint against the cultural relativism put forth in ethnological research. Secondly – this is our new loose end that can be noted here only in passing – the critique of relativism both in Merleau-Ponty and Aron is informed by the critical reflection on the definition and limits of scientific, or more broadly, rational »objectivity« as universally valid predication on principles, insights, and values. The investigation about the »objective« nature of values as universal values orienting human culture in history places the discussion of relativism squarely in the complex context of the epistemological, methodological, ontological, and axiological research of German neocritical philosophy of the first decades of the twentieth century. The focus on the limits of objectivity of historical knowledge in connection with notions of value, interest, selection becomes in both authors the starting point for a renewed probing of the traditional definition of the human being as rational and for integrating the modern project of a philosophical anthropology into a sustained and still compelling meditation on the evolutionary conception of history.[18]

à la question de l'événement: l'institution en effet est avant tout un événement et de l'événement elle possède certains caractères fondamentaux, à savoir la singularité, la facticité, la fécondité, l'anonymat. 2) *La référence à l'ouverture d'un champ de reprises et de transformations* ou, du point de vue historique, *d'une tradition*. Et un point essentiel consiste en ceci, que *ces deux pôles doivent toujours être pensés ensemble,* comme les deux faces d'un même phénomène enchevêtrées dans des relations multiples. C'est justement l'articulation explicite de ces relations multiples qui permet de montrer l'institution historique comme une voie pour penser l'événement historique.« Terzi 2017, 8.

18 Merleau-Ponty's critique of cultural relativism in the lecture course on »Institution« makes explicit reference to the work of Max Weber. See Merleau-Ponty 2010 [2003], 13. The extensive critical reassessment of the problem of Marxist politics and philosophy of history in *Les adventures de la dialectique* not only mentions Aron in the preface with the aim to capture the main thesis of the whole book but also begins with a study on Weber's historical analyses and the theory of historical understanding to be drawn from them. See Merleau-Ponty 1964 [1955], 9–29. Merleau-Ponty also gave a course at the Collège de France in 1953–54 with the title »Materials for a Theory of History« that develops the theme of history again starting with a study of Weber's work as outlining a »phenomenology of historical choices.« The course also takes up a reading of Georg Lukács' *Geschichte und Klassenbewusstsein* from 1923 with the

References

Aron, Raymond. 1948 [1938]. *Introduction à la philosophie de l'histoire*. Gallimard, Paris.
—. 1964. »The Rationality of Modern Society«, in *Bulletin of the Atomic Scientists*. Vol. XX, N° 1.
—. 1970. »Le Paradoxe du même et de l'autre«, in *Échanges et communications*, ed. J. Pouillon and P. Maranda, *Studies in Genetal Anthropology*, V. Vol. II. The Hague, Mouton.
—. 2011 [1946]. »La Philosophie de l'histoire«, in *Dimensions de la conscience historique*. Paris, Les Belles Lettres.
—. 2011 [1957]. »La notion du sens de l'histoire«, in *Dimensions de la conscience historique*. Paris, Les Belles Lettres.
—. 2011 [1959]. »De l'objet de l'histoire«, in *Dimensions de la conscience historique*. Paris, Les Belles Lettres.
—. 2011 [1960]. »L'aube de l'histoire universelle«, in *Dimensions de la conscience historique*. Paris, Les Belles Lettres.
Bimbenet, Etienne. 2004. *Nature et Humanité. Merleau-Ponty – le problèbe anthropologique*. Paris, Vrin.
Broekman, Jan M. 1971, *Strukturalismus*. Freiburg / München, Verlag Karl Alber.
Bruzina, Ronald. 1981. »Dependence on Language and Autonomy of Reason«, in *Man and World*, 14.
—. 2001. »Construction in Phenomenology«, in *The Reach of Reflection: Issues for Phenomenology's Second Century*. Steven Crowell, Lester Embress, Samuel J. Julian (eds.). Center for Advanced Research in Phenomenology.
Goldman, Marcio. 2004. »Lévi-Strauss et les sens de l'histoire«, in *Les temps modernes*, Vol. 628. Issue 3.
Jacquet-Francillon, François. 2017. »Questions à l'anti-humanisme de Claude Lévi-Strauss«, in *Le Télémaque*, 2, N° 52. Presses universitaires de Caen.
Lévi-Strauss, Claude. 1963 [1949]. »History and Anthropology«, in *Structural Anthropology*. Basic Books.
—. 1983 [1952]. »Race and History«, in *Structural Anthropology. Volume 2*. Chicago, The University of Chicago Press.
—. 1983 [1956]. »The Three Humanisms«, *Structural Anthropology. Volume 2*. Chicago, The University of Chicago Press.
—. 2021 [1962]. *Wild Thought*. Chicago, The University of Chicago Press.
Merleau-Ponty, Maurice. 1964 [1947]. »The Metaphysical in Man«, in *Sense and Non-Sense*. Evanston, IL, Northwestern University Press.

---

aim to relaunch the critical questioning of »the Marxist idea of a meaning which is immanent in history.« See Merleau-Ponty 1970 [1968], 27–38. The confrontation with the neocritical philosophy of history is to be found everywhere in Aron, starting with his early studies on *La théorie de l'histoire dans l'Allemagne contemporaine. La philosophie critique de l'histoire* (1938) and *Introduction à la philosophie de l'histoire. Essai sur les limites de l'objectivité historique* (1938).

—. 1964 [1962]. »An Unpublished Text by Maurice Merleau-Ponty: A Prospectus of His Work«, in *The Primacy of Perception*. Evanston, IL, Northwestern University Press.
—. 1964 [1959]. »Form Mauss to Claude Lévi-Strauss«, in *Signs*. Evanston, IL, Northwestern University Press.
—. 1968 [1964]. *The Visible and the Invisible*. Evanston, IL, Northwestern University Press.
—. 1970 [1968]. *Themes from the Lectures*. Evanston, IL, Northwestern University Press.
—. 1973 [1955]. *The Adventures of Dialectic*. Evanston, IL, Northwestern University Press.
—. 2010 [2003]. *Institution and Passivity: Course Notes from the Collège de France (1954–1955)*. Evanston, IL, Northwestern University Press.
—. 2012 [1945]. *Phenomenology of Perception*. Routledge, London and New York.
Terzi, Roberto. 2017. »Institution, événement et histoire chez Merleau-Ponty«, in *Bulletin*
d'analyse phénoménologique, XIII, 3.

Roberto Redaelli

Artificial Intelligence and Quasi-Normativity: Some Indications for a Solution to the Normative Question in the Field of AI Ethics

1. Normativity: from humans to artificial intelligence

Today, many disciplines are devoting special attention from a variety of perspectives to the normative nature of our forms of life. From linguistics to jurisprudence, from anthropology to philosophy, from economics to neuroscience, the subject of normativity constitutes a Gordian knot of the present age, towards which the efforts of scientific and philosophical understanding are directed. Emblematic of the growing interest in this topic is the flourishing of numerous theories of normativity, which are based, in the field of philosophy, on thinkers of both the present and the past. In fact, alongside normative theories that appeal to phenomenology (see, e.g., Smith 2012; Crowell 2013, 2019; Loidolt 2019; Heinämaa et al. 2022) or philosophical anthropology (see, e.g., Schloßberger 2019), a number of theoretical proposals stand out on the current philosophical horizon that draw on the thought of Aristotle (see, e.g., LeBar 2008), Hegel and Kant, to name but a few examples. This is why the *vexata questio* still echoes today in various areas of philosophy, this time in reference to the normative sphere: Aristotle or Plato? Kant or Hegel?[1]

With regard to this last question, at least in the field of analytic ethics, Kant's work seems to have a certain pre-eminence. Indeed, though accused by the opposing currents of formalism and individualism, his work has, in recent years, been given a prominent place, making the philosopher from Königsberg a key reference point for all those who approach the problems of ethics and metaethics. As we are well aware, this veritable Kant-Renaissance was initiated

[1] The question is posed by Krijnen (2019).

by Rawls' essay *Kantian Constructivism in Moral Theory* (1980), which inaugurated the theoretical position that, naturally, was called constructivism. According to this position, »insofar as there are normative truths, they are not fixed by normative facts that are independent of what rational agents would agree to under some specified conditions of choice« (Bagnoli 2017).

One of Rawls' most promising pupils, Christine Korsgaard, has adhered to this position, which has evolved in numerous Kantian and non-Kantian forms. Korsgaard is credited with initiating, at the Tanner Lectures on Human Values in 1992, a heated debate on what the sources of moral normativity are. The philosopher has, in fact, placed at the centre of her lectures what she has grouped under the title of normative question, expressing it in various forms: What justifies the claims that morality makes on us? Is there anything we must do?

A number of leading representatives of today's diverse philosophical panorama have debated over the answer offered by Korsgaard to these questions – an answer that appeals to the Kantian notion of autonomy and the distinctly existentialist concept of practical identity. Alongside the observations of G.A. Cohen, R. Geuss, T. Nagel and B. Williams, which have constituted a commentary on Korsgaard's Tanner Lectures, more recent remarks of a phenomenological and hermeneutic nature have been added, through which an attempt has been made to understand the origin of the cogent force of moral reasons, and thus of their ability to guide our actions. But, in addition to the various responses offered by philosophical enquiry, there are others that, although not directly addressed to Korsgaard's text, have transcended the boundaries of the purely philosophical debate and invested disparate fields of enquiry.[2] Some of them have revitalised the ambitious Nietzschean project of tracing a genealogy of morality. This genealogy has nowadays sometimes taken on a phylogenetic point of view, based on a natural history of human morality (see, e.g., Tomasello 2016), and sometimes an ontogenetic perspective, either sociological or based on the findings of child psychology (see, e.g., Fittipaldi 2012; Tomasello 2019). In these cases, psychologists, sociologists and anthropologists have sought to identify the various sources of normativity, highlighting the role played, in the process of emergence of the normative sphere, by phenomena such as coopera-

2 For an overview of different scientific perspectives that investigate the normative question see, e.g., Funke and Redaelli (2021).

tion (see, e.g., Tomasello 2009), education and aggression (see, e.g., Wrangham 2019).

Enriching the framework traced by such investigations aimed directly (or indirectly) at the normative question is the problem of the moral status of artificial agents and the moral value of their actions. Artificial intelligence systems in particular raise increasingly urgent ethical issues, necessitating a discussion that considers the moral status not only of the living (human and non-human beings), but also of the non-living things, and in this case of the technological object, too, with its (possible) capacity to convey normative demands. It is to this capacity that this paper is devoted, aiming to understand the origin and nature of the binding force conveyed by AI. To this purpose, it is first necessary to present the normative question posed by Korsgaard and to offer an overview of the main theories concerning the sources of moral normativity. With such an overview we wish to trace in advance the boundaries within which our investigation of the moral capacity of AI will take place (par. 2). Within these boundaries, we then intend to focus on the merits and limits of the recent treatment of digital normativity proposed by Fourneret and Yvert (par. 3), and finally, bring a decisive correction to their considerations by introducing the notion of quasi-normativity (par. 4 & 5). In order to introduce and develop this notion in the context of enquiry into the digital sphere, we will make use of Don Ihde's postphenomenological considerations on the nature of the artificial agent as a quasi-other. Thanks to these insights and the introduction of the notion of quasi-normativity, we believe it is possible to shed new light on the binding force of AI.

2. The normative question: some preliminary remarks

The problem of moral normativity raised by Korsgaard concerns the source of the authority of our moral standards, of their ability to guide our actions. What is at stake with this question is, more precisely, the origin of the force they exert on us in the intricate network of our everyday lives. For Korsgaard, in fact, moral reasons do not have a descriptive nature, but rather a prescriptive one, which prompts the agent, confronted with their authority, to raise questions about their justification. Hence, in the face of the pressing demands that morality makes on us, the question arises: why should I be moral? (Korsgaard 1996, 9)

This question opens up a constellation of problems concerning the right of morality to impose laws on us; a right that, it should be made clear from the outset, has very little to do with the question of whether and why it is *convenient* for us to be moral (Korsgaard 1996, 9). In fact, the authority of morality that Korsgaard seeks is unconditional, that is, independent of whether or not its injunctions are corroborated by our interests and inclinations. Thus posed, the normative question distances itself, on the one hand, from any form of utilitarianism, while on the other hand, it embraces Kant's search for the unconditioned, with which the philosopher intends to put an end to moral scepticism, which endlessly repeats the question »why must I do that?«. Korsgaard succeeds in identifying this unconditioned not through an appeal to some intrinsically normative entity, but through recourse to what she defines in terms of reflexive approval. The normative question therefore evaluates the authority of morality, avoiding bringing into play both some form of substantive realism[3] and any version of utilitarianism: it is answered by a Kantianism that is, so to speak, existential[4], as we shall now see.

Precisely because of the peculiar approach taken to the normative question and the theoretical force of her constructivism, Korsgaard's philosophical proposal has had and continues to have a loud echo in the multifaceted contemporary philosophical panorama, within which it is possible to recognise three different approaches used to address this question. W.H. Smith has offered a valuable overview of these approaches (Smith 2012, 6–7), which we would like to take up here, if only schematically, in order to define in advance the coordinates within which our investigation into the moral normativity of AI will be carried out.

---

3 Unlike substantive realism, whereby there are values out there that can be intuitively perceived, Korsgaard defines her philosophical position in terms of procedural realism: »the form of realism I am endorsing here is a procedural rather than substantive realism: values are constructed by a procedure, the procedure of making laws for ourselves« (Korsgaard 1996, 112).

4 Responding to Nagel's remarks, Korsgaard confesses in *The Sources of Normativity* that »Nagel also makes this point, characterizing my appeal to identity as ›rather existentialist‹ (I think correctly) and also as therefore unKantian (I think incorrectly)« (Korsgaard 1996, 237).

The first approach, which is the one employed by Korsgaard, is defined by the author herself in the *first person*. In it, an internalist perspective is taken, characterised grammatically by the use of the pronoun ›I‹. Here, it must be clarified why a certain reason is binding to the first person, i.e. from the subjective perspective of the agent. In order to offer an adequate answer to this question, Korsgaard appeals, as just mentioned, to a specific human characteristic, that of self-reflection.[5] Unlike non-human animals, which act in accordance with their desires and instincts without these instincts being the object of attention and deliberation, man cannot be content with such incentives, but needs reasons to believe and to act. Such reasons, for Korsgaard, are nothing other than a type of reflective success,[6] i.e. our perceptions and desires provide reasons if they pass the test of reflective scrutiny:[7] it is, in fact, »in the internal world created by self-consciousness, that reason is born« (Korsgaard 2009, 116). Reflection thus seems to free the human subject from the authority of instincts that dominates the animal kingdom and at the same time opens up a normative space in which the human subject binds himself to his/her own moral standards. In this sense, Korsgaard in her argument calls into play the Kantian notion of autonomy, while recognising autonomy as only a formal condition for moral action. Alongside autonomy, the author in fact adds the notion of practical identities, understood as »self-images founded in the concrete life forms« (Staiti 2015, 172). Such practical identities (such as father, mother, husband, teacher) provide »constitutive standards« with respect to which we can fail or succeed, or more accurately, standards in the light of which our reasons and obligations arise. Clearly this first-person perspective, combining autonomy and practical identity, has the limitation, underlined by several critics (see, e.g., Smith 2012, 34–42; Crowell

---

5 The notion of self-reflection called into question by Korsgaard has been the subject of pressing criticism, including that of Mark Okrent, echoed in part by Steven Crowell. According to Okrent, the notion of self-reflection as presented by Korsgaard gives rise to three different interpretations, leaving this notion for the most part undefined (Okrent 1999; Crowell 2013, 246 ff).

6 From this perspective, Korsgaard observes, »scepticism about the good and the right is not scepticism about the existence of intrinsically normative entities. It is the view that the problems which reflection sets for us are insoluble, that the questions to which it gives rise have no answers« (Korsgaard 1996, 94).

7 More precisely, Korsgaard states that »each impulse as it offers itself to the will must pass a kind of test for normativity before we can adopt it as a reason for action« (Korsgaard 1996, 91).

2013, 246 ff), of not accounting for the normative force of the other: the other, the ›you‹, is reduced, as Smith correctly observed, to »a source of proto-moral reasons – analogous to bodily incentives or inclinations in practical deliberation« (Smith 2012, 37).

In contrast to Korsgaard's approach, the second-person perspective, which Smith also espouses, is characterised by the point of view of the ›you‹, where it is no longer the ›I‹ addressing itself, but rather the encounter with the ›other‹ that is pre-eminent. In this perspective, the cogent force of moral injunction does not arise from self-reflection, but rather originally from the appeal, from the question that the other addresses to the self. It is a matter here, in Levinassian terms, of a face-to-face encounter with the other and a consequent interpersonal foundation of morality, which has taken and continues to take disparate forms, sometimes radically different from one another, such as those proposed by Darwall (2006), Crowell and Smith himself. While Darwall appeals to Kant and emphasises a symmetry between the ›I‹ and the ›you‹, Crowell elaborates a second-person phenomenology (see Crowell 2015, 2019), with which he emphasises in Levinassian terms a dissymmetry between the ›I‹ and the ›other‹.

Referring specifically to Smith, it can be observed that following Crowell's line of thought, he attempts to elaborate a theory that harmoniously brings together a normative first-person moment and a second-person perspective. In this way, Smith intends to give an ontological foundation to Levinas' vis-a-vis reflection through recourse to Heidegger's notions of *Mitsein* and resoluteness. By virtue of this intermingling, this position assigns a central ethical role to the other, without for that reason diminishing the importance of the first-person moment.

The third-person perspective is, on the other hand, the one embodied by the figure of the disinterested spectator, who observes, so to speak, from outside, from nowhere, what happens in the world. This perspective is adopted, paradigmatically, in the field of science, where an objective view of the world is pursued. In the field of ethics, one of the greatest representatives of this approach is, as is well known, Thomas Nagel, whose thinking leads to a form of realism, according to which there are agent-neutral reasons: from the objectivity of these reasons derives their normative force. In this and other forms of realism, the normative question seems, however, to become less interesting since the answer to this question, as Wedgwood states,

»corresponds to an appropriate normative truth or fact« (Wedgwood 2007, 7).

Once we have broadly outlined the framework within which we intend to place our reflections on AI, it is appropriate to recall the recent considerations of Fourneret and Yvert (2020), which have the merit of illuminating the normative issue in relation to AI. These considerations will constitute the starting point for our own reflection, which aims to enrich and supplement the authors' position. To this end, we shall first resort to certain instances present in the debate on the sources of moral normativity recalled here briefly and then introduce, from a postphenomenological perspective, the notion of quasi-normativity.

3. Digital normativity & artificial intelligence

The pervasive presence of AI systems in our lives is giving rise to what has been defined by Fourneret and Yvert as forms of digital normativity. By this expression, the authors mean »the ability of algorithms to establish standards that humans incorporate as what should be considered as normal in their lives and guide their actions« (Fourneret and Yvert 2020, 1). These AI-originated standards thus have a normative power, i.e. the ability to guide, to incline our actions and beliefs. They are not a mere description of what we already do and believe, but rather aim to make us act in certain directions. Algorithms are, in fact, able to retrieve trends that they recognise in the data they possess and thus create »a normalized view« of the problems they face (Fourneret and Yvert 2020). In the terminology of the debate we have just gone over, we could say that these algorithms give us reasons to act and decide in certain situations.[8]

For Fourneret and Yvert, the first form of digital normativity is closely related to a second one, which involves predictive algorithms in particular. These algorithms suggest certain behaviours on the basis of our previous behaviour and that of other users, without any consideration of the reasons for our behaviour. In this way the

[8] It should be emphasised here that the action of technological artefacts is not susceptible to reasons explanation and therefore, as Johnson notes, they are not moral agents (Johnson 2006). However, this limitation does not prevent these artificial agents from offering reasons for human action and beliefs.

individual is »objectivized (normalized) by the algorithm« (Fourneret and Yvert 2020, 1). In line with the first form of digital normativity, which creates a normalised view of the problems for which AI was created, the second form leads to a normalised view of ourselves. In this sense, the algorithm reduces the individual and his behaviour to his data (and the data of other individuals), without any consideration of the motivations for his behaviour and the ethical scope of his actions. This second form of digital normativity has a recursive and dynamic character, which in our view is also present in the first, whereby »algorithmic recommendations emanating from previous human actions in turn influence their next actions« (Fourneret and Yvert 2020, 2).

A third form of digital normativity derives from the predictive *efficiency* of algorithms. This capacity now surpasses in many fields that of humans, imposing norms to which humans adapt. This subordination to the effectiveness of the algorithms occurs even when the process by which the system arrived at the result is unclear. This raises the problem of moral and legal responsibility for the effects produced by AI. Precisely in order to deal with the so-called black box problem, there is a tendency today to point to transparency as indispensable value for the development of a trustworthy AI. In this sense, it has been proposed to introduce checkpoints and/or the repetition of stress-tests in intelligent systems.[9]

Now, the important thing to emphasise about the considerations made by Fourneret and Yvert is the role that, according to the authors, these types of digital normativity can play within the complex process of human subjectivation, whereby this term is understood to mean the »construction process leading someone to become and be aware of being a subject, i.e., being free and responsible for one's actions and at the foundation of one's representations and judgments« (Fourneret and Yvert 2020, 2).

For the authors, in fact, AI systems are capable of exerting a decisive influence on the process of subjectivation, according to a twofold dynamic: on the one hand, they can help us to stop performing certain burdensome tasks, but on the other hand, they can also lead us to stop making decisions in certain areas of our lives due to the predictive effectiveness of algorithms. One example that has become famous is that of the judge who in some legal systems uses algorithms

[9] On this point, see Cristianini (2023, here: 155–159).

to determine the risk of recidivism. In this case, a conflict could arise between the judge's decision and that of the algorithm, or as in the Compas case,[10] there could be biases that negatively influence the judge's decision supported by intelligent systems.

Beyond these limitations, the extraordinary possibilities offered by predictive algorithms, according to the authors' diagnosis, could activate in future generations an »AI governmentality« (Fourneret and Yvert 2020, 2) with a consequent process of de-empowerment, whereby humans would blindly rely on the results obtained by intelligent systems. In fact, although our ability to resist the normative force arising from models established by AI always remains open (Fourneret and Yvert 2020, 2), the effectiveness of this technology could ultimately lead to an imposition, albeit non-violent, of the AI's choices. Such an imposition would take place, and already does, through a radical change in our practices of living and knowing. Faced with this risk, the authors suggest accompanying the development of AI with an ethical reflection such as the one promoted by P.P. Verbeek, which, at the level of design, identifies the value system of which the technology is the bearer and reflects on the principles to be followed to protect the process of subjectivation.

In order to highlight the strengths and shortcomings of Fourneret and Yvert's succinct considerations, it is now necessary to read the proposal put forward by the authors in the light of certain elements of the first- and second-person theories we mentioned in the previous section. First of all, artificial intelligence, by virtue of its effectiveness, makes demands with a normative character to which man is called upon to respond. In this sense, AI is recognised as the other that presents itself to the self, so that in the encounter with the face of the other, as Levinas argues and Smith emphasises, there is an ethical interdiction or the calling into question of my freedom. The authors respond to this calling into question of human freedom by appealing to an ethics of design that clearly performs the function of self-reflection proposed by Korsgaard's theory. According to this theory, the demands of the other need to pass reflexive scrutiny in order to become reasons for the ›I‹ to act and believe.

Following this direction of enquiry, one can thus recognise in Fourneret and Yvert's thought processes a second-person perspective, whereby moral normativity arises in the face-to-face with the other,

---

[10] For the Compas case, see Brennan et al. (2009).

and a first-person moment, whereby the other's injunction has no normative force until it obtains the ›I‹'s approval. From the intertwining of these two moments two crucial questions stand out clearly, the resolution of which can help clarify the nature of digital normativity. The first question concerns the perception of AI as the other: can the AI be treated as the other (a human or non-human being)? And if the answer is yes, then do AI's injunctions to act have the same normative force as human ones? This last part of the first question is closely linked to the second question concerning the nature of digital normativity: can one base the normative force of the demands made by AI on mere efficiency, thus according to a utilitarian perspective that Korsgaard's Kantian position seems to oust from moral discourse?

In order to answer the first question, i.e. the problem of the identification of AI with the other, we shall make use of Ihde's postphenomenological analyses of the mediating role played by technologies in our lives, while for the resolution of the second question we shall employ the notion of proto-normativity or quasi-normativity, which we have already developed elsewhere (see, e.g., Redaelli 2021) and which we feel it useful to recall here in order to clarify what links (legitimately or illegitimately) the normative force of AI to efficiency.

4. Artificial intelligence from a postphenomenological perspective and the notion of quasi-normativity. Some indications for a solution to the normative question in the field of AI ethics

The postphenomenological approach inaugurated by Ihde has the undisputed merit of combining philosophical analysis and empirical investigation in the search for the relationships between human beings and technological artefacts[11]. In this type of inquiry, Ihde makes a decisive contribution to Science and Technology Studies (STS) by highlighting different forms of technological mediation. For the author, in fact, technologies mediate our relationship to the world in a polyform manner and direct our actions. By virtue of this role, the human-world relationship typically assumes the form ›human-technology-world‹.

[11] An accurate introduction to postphenomenology can be found in Rosenberger/Verbeek (2015), 9–41.

Ihde's thinking is now renowned, so a synoptical outline of the major notions of his proposal is herein satisfactory. As we know, Ihde identifies four forms of technological mediation: embodiment relations, hermeneutic relations, background relations, and alterity relations. This list, as we shall now see, is not meant to be exhaustive, and one form of mediation does not exclude the other, so the same technology can realise different forms of mediation.

The first type of human-technology relationship is characterised by the fact that, as the philosopher states, »I take the technologies *into* my experiencing in a particular way by way of perceiving *through* such technologies and through the reflexive transformation of my perceptual and body sense« (Ihde 1990, 72). In this relationship, therefore, technology becomes an extension of the human body, it becomes a quasi-me. Examples of this kind of relationship are offered by optical technologies such as the telescope or eyeglasses. Both play a mediating role between the seer and the seen, whereby »one sees *through* the optics« (Ihde 1990, 73). The same can be said for hearing aids that become an extension of one's body. However, regardless of the different type of technology used, what characterises, according to Ihde, the *embodiment* relationship is the fact that the technology involved in such a relationship must somehow withdraw from our attention in order to be incorporated. Therefore, the closer the technology is to transparency, the more it allows the extension of one's own bodily sense (Ihde 1990, 74).

The second type of human-technology relationship is defined by Ihde in terms of a hermeneutic relationship. In this case, in short, technologies offer a representation of the world that requires interpretation. For this reason, Ihde speaks of a *hermeneutic* relation explicitly referring to the study of interpretation. An example is provided by the thermometer that allows us to »read« temperature through numbers (Ihde 1990, 85).

Another type of relation identified by the philosopher is the *background* relation. In this type of relation, technology gives form to our environment, although it is, so to speak, *unthematised*. The thermostat that regulates the temperature in the room and the bright light that allows us to see the objects around us are both part of our environment, although we do not have a direct relationship with these technologies. They remain in the *background*.

The last type of relationship is the one we wish to focus on most because it explicitly involves artificial intelligence: it is the *alterity* relationship. In this type of relationship, technology does not mediate our relationship to the world, rather we establish a relationship *with or to* technology (Ihde 1990, 97). Therefore, in this case, technology is the *terminus* of the relationship: technologies emerge as focal entities.

Taking the term alterity from Levinas to denote the radical difference that separates every man from every other man, Ihde (1990, 98, 102) defines, within the alterity relation, technology as a quasi-other, referring to AI specifically in such terms. While pointing out the risks of anthropomorphizing technology by recognising a quasi-other in it, Ihde (1990, 103) emphasises that the automaton exemplified by a robot is a quasi-other to which we can pay attention, because although the robot has a different experience of the world than we do,[12] it presents itself as the other end of a possible social relation.

In order to support his argument, Ihde also cites the example of the video game, which involves not only a relationship of embodiment (»the joystick that embodies hand«) and hermeneutics (the context of the game, e.g. some sport analogue), but also the sense of »*interacting with* something other than me, the technological *competitor*« (1990, 100). In the competition that materialises in the video game there is, in fact, an exchange or dialogue with the quasi-other.

In terms of the dialogue between man and machine, in order to better understand the alterity relation, we can think not only of robots, but also of the chatbots with which most of us now interact on a daily basis. These technologies, exemplified by digital assistants, simulate different types of conversations, respond to our requests and increasingly customise their activities according to our preferences. They apply predictive intelligence and perform an analysis of huge amounts of data through which they are able to offer us increasingly accurate suggestions, anticipating our needs. Precisely because of these characteristics, we could say that we perceive such chatbots as quasi-others in the same way as Ihde has referred to robots. In fact, (ro)bots,[13] as just mentioned, although they are not human, do not appear to us as mere tools: they are something other than us, an ›other than us‹ with whom we can have a social relationship. Robots and

---

12 Ihde (1990, 103) emphasises the difference between humans and robots, highlighting how the robot's „experience" of the world is significantly different from the human experience already at a sensory level.

13 We make use here of the spelling used by Wallach and Allen to refer to both robots and chatbots. See Wallach and Allen (2009).

chatbots co-form our practices of living and knowing with a degree of autonomy, adaptability and interaction[14] that other tools do not have. We need only think of the extreme cases of care robots or sex robots with which individuals have relationships involving the affective sphere, or some types of chatbots that are so advanced that it is difficult to understand whether we are interacting with a human or an artificial agent.

Starting from this characterisation of robots and chatbots, we can now elaborate on a crucial point developed by Fourneret and Yvert that is linked to the question of digital normativity. Synthesising the authors' thinking, we could say that the higher the efficiency of robots in relating to us, the more the responses and demands they make will have normative force, i.e. the force to direct our actions.[15] And similarly, the more satisfactory the predictive capacity of AI, the more we will trust the results it returns, up to the point where we blindly accept the results obtained from AI. In this sense, certainly Fourneret and Yvert are right in linking the normative capacity of AI to its efficiency, with a consequent risk to the process of subjectivation. And yet, while, according to the authors, the efficiency of intelligent systems lends normative force to the results they obtain, the possibility of taking a position in the face of such results remains open (Fourneret and Yvert 2020, 2). This capacity, mentioned by the authors only in passing and implicit in the appeal to ethics, actually shows how the efficiency-normativity link does not entirely resolve the normative issue in intelligent systems. In fact, if one understands normativity as the cogent force, that is, the authority that the standards (which may or may not be moral) created by predictive systems exert on us, giving us reasons to act in certain directions, it can be observed that the instances promoted by AI do not give rise to a pure form of normativity, because this only occurs after passing the test of reflection. Instead, they give rise to what we propose to call, in accordance with Ihde's terminology, quasi-normative instances, with the ›quasi‹ here indicating that such instances are not normative in the full sense, but neither are they morally neutral. They are, in fact, characterised by the fact that, although they require our approval in order to be normative in the strict sense, they already possess

14 Although there is no consensus definition of AI, it is customary to recognise autonomy, interactivity and adaptability as characteristics of intelligent systems.

15 In this sense, one could observe that the moral authority of AI can derive solely from the efficiency of its predictions and actions.

an injunctive force, linked to the predictive efficiency of algorithms, that redefines to a certain degree our space of freedom and directs our action.

An example proving the validity of this thesis, according to which AI is the bearer of a quasi-normative and *not* normative instance in the strict sense, is offered to us in the postphenomenological field by P.P. Verbeek who, in the opening of his *Moralizing Technology*, introduces his proposal – that technologies have moral significance as mediators – from the effects of the use of certain medical devices. A good example is obstetric ultrasonography (see Verbeek 2008b, 2011).[16] For the philosopher, one cannot attribute to this technology a merely functional role (that of making visible an unborn child in the womb), but rather it redefines both the ontological status of the child and our experience thereof. Indeed, such technology, capable of predicting whether the child will be affected by certain diseases or not, transforms the child into a possible patient and its parents into makers of decisions about its life. In this way, medical devices redefine the relationship between child and parents in hitherto unexpected terms, whereby pregnancy becomes a process of choice (Verbeek 2011, 25). In fact, the possibility to have »sonograms made, and therefore to detect congenital defects before birth irreversibly changes the character of what used to be called ›expecting a child‹« (Verbeek 2011, 25). In our terms, we could say that such technology is the bearer of quasi-normative demands, i.e. having a certain capacity to direct action; these demands, as already mentioned, can only become normative, i.e. binding, with human approval. In fact, while we only need to consider that since the introduction of these technologies, the very choice not to have an ultrasound scan made is also a choice, on the other hand, even in the case of serious illnesses diagnosed in the unborn child, these predictive systems do not exert such a coercive force on the parents that they are induced to abort. In this case, therefore, while it is clear that the redefinition of reality by technologies entails the emergence of a quasi-normativity – in this case, a push to choose that was not as strong before the introduction of such devices –, on the other hand, it is even clearer that any predictions that emerge from the use of such technologies lack the authority possessed by normative issues subjected to the scrutiny of reflection.

16 On the use of AI in prenatal diagnosis see He et al. (2021).

5. Brief conclusions: the hybrid origin of normativity and AI

In light of these considerations, it can be observed that the emergence of normativity, as a binding force prescribing a certain behaviour to the subject, is not attributable to technology alone but is the effect of the interrelation between non-humans and humans. In this sense, according to our hermeneutic hypothesis, normativity is inextricably linked to the quasi-normative sphere of technological apparatus, without, however, imputing to the latter a role other than that of mediation ascribed to it by Verbeek (2008a) and before him, by Ihde.[17] In this sense, it can be observed that the normative force of reasons has a relational character, so to speak: it has its terrain of origin in the relationship between self and other or, in the case of AI, quasi-other. And it is precisely this relationship, we may add as an afterword to our discourse, that gives rise to a ›we-society‹ composed today not only of human and non-human living beings, but also of some artificial intelligent systems. The latter are in fact part of our society, they are quasi-others, because the relationships we have with them clearly share with other types of social relationships the fact that they, in the words of Margalit and Raz, »depend for their existence on the sharing of patterns of expectations, on traditions preserving implicit knowledge of how to do what, of tacit conventions regarding what is part of this or that enterprise and what is not, what is appropriate and what is not, what is valuable and what is not« (Margalit and Raz 1990). In this precise sense, intelligent systems are products of our society, of which they are the spokesmen, and hence the need for that appeal to the ethics of design that allows us to decide what values these robots *should* contain and represent; a decision that protects our process of subjectivation, albeit only in part, from the risks of degeneration highlighted by Fourneret and Yvert. In fact, as long as the disruptive force of AI is recognised as a form of quasi-normativity, man will always remain responsible for the standards he intends to adopt, and the efficacy of AI itself cannot replace human intelligence;

---

17 It should also be noted here that the models proposed by the algorithms are extrapolated from our data and the algorithms themselves are produced by us. Therefore, from a genetic point of view, it can be observed that the instances raised by AI are already a product of the interrelation between man and technology. In order to understand this interrelation between humans and technology, one refers in the postphenomenological field to the notion of composite intentionality (see Verbeek 2011). On the notion of composite intentionality in the field of AI see Redaelli (2023).

if anything, it can enhance it by expanding the human field of freedom and responsibility. In this sense, paraphrasing the famous words of G. Anders, the possibilities opened up by technology, and more specifically by AI, *do not have to* be realised, but rather *remain open possibilities on which we have to take a stand* in the ongoing process of human self-formation.

References

Bagnoli, C. (2017). Constructivism in metaethics. In: Zalta, E. N. (Ed), *The stanford encyclopedia of philosophy* (Winter 2017 edn).

Brennan, T., Dieterich, W., Ehret, B (2009). Evaluating the predictive validity of the COMPAS risk and needs assessment system. *Crim Justice Behav* 36, 21–40. https://doi.org/10.1177/0093854808326545

Cristianini, N. (2023). *The shortcut: why intelligent machines do not think like us*. Boca Raton/London/New York: CRC Press.

Crowell, S. (2013). *Normativity and phenomenology in Husserl and Heidegger*. Cambridge: Cambridge University Press.

Crowell, S. (2015). Second-person phenomenology. In: Szanto, T., Moran, D. (Eds), *Phenomenology of sociality. Discovering the ›we‹*, 70–89. New York: Routledge.

Crowell, S. (2019). Second-person reasons: Darwall, Levinas, and the phenomenology of reason. In: Fagenblat, M., Erdur, M. (Eds.), *Levinas and analytic philosophy: second-person normativity and the moral life*, 4–28. New York: Routledge.

Darwall, S. (2006). *The second-person standpoint: morality, respect, and accountability*. Cambridge: Harvard University Press.

Fittipaldi, E. (2012). *Everyday legal ontology*. Milano: LED.

Fourneret, E., Yvert, B. (2020). Digital Normativity: a challenge for human subjectivation. *Front Artif Intell* 3:27. https://doi.org/10.3389/frai.2020.00027

Funke, A., Redaelli, R. (2021). Rethinking the sources of normativity in ethics. *Ethics & Politics* 2: 257–260.

He, F., Wang, Y., Xiu, Y., Zhang, Y., Chen, L. (2021). Artificial intelligence in prenatal ultrasound diagnosis. *Front Med* 8:729978. https://doi.org/10.3389/fmed.2021.729978

Heinämaa, S., Hartimo, M., Hirvonen, I. (2022). *Contemporary phenomenologies of normativity: norms, goals, and values*. New York: Routledge.

Ihde, D. (1990). *Technology and the lifeworld: from garden to earth*. Bloomington and Indianapolis: Indiana University Press.

Johnson, D. G. (2006). Computer systems: moral entities but not moral agents. *Ethics Inf Technol* 8: 195–204. https://doi.org/10.1007/s10676-006-9111-5

Korsgaard, C. M. (1996). *The sources of normativity*. New York: Cambridge University Press.

Korsgaard, C. M. (2009). *Self-constitution: agency, identity, and integrity*. Oxford: Oxford University Press.
Krijnen, C. (2019). *Concepts of normativity: Kant or Hegel?* Leiden: Brill.
LeBar, M. (2008). Aristotelian constructivism. *Soc Philos Policy* 25: 182–213. https://doi.org/10.1017/S0265052508080072
Loidolt, S. (2019). Experience and normativity: the phenomenological approach. In: Cimino, A., Leijenhorst, C. (Eds), *Phenomenology and experience: new perspectives*. Leiden and Boston: Brill.
Margalit, A., Raz, J. (1990). National self-determination. *J Philos* 87: 439–461. https://doi.org/10.2307/2026968
Okrent, M. (1999). Heidegger and Korsgaard on human reflection. *Philos Top*, 27: 47–76. https://doi.org/10.5840/philtopics19992724
Rawls, J. (1980). Kantian constructivism in moral theory. *J Philos*, 77: 515–572. https://doi.org/10.2307/2025790
Redaelli, R. (2021). A relational account of moral normativity: the Neo-Kantian notion of we-subject. *J Transcend Philos* 2: 303–320. https://doi.org/10.1515/jtph-2021-0014.
Redaelli, R. (2023). From tool to mediator. A postphenomenological approach to artificial intelligence. In: Possati, L. (Ed), *Humanizing Artificial Intelligence: Psychoanalysis and the Problem of Control*. Berlin: De Gruyter.
Rosenberger, R., Verbeek P.-P. (2015). A Field Guide to Postphenomenology. In: Rosenberger, R., Verbeek, P.-P. (Eds.), *Postphenomenological Investigations: Essays on Human-Technology Relations*, 9–41. London: Lexington Books.
Schloßberger, M. (2019). *Phänomenologie der Normativität. Entwurf einer materialen Anthropologie im Anschluss an Max Scheler und Helmuth Plessner*. Basel: Schwabe.
Smith, W. H. (2012). *The phenomenology of moral normativity*. London and New York: Routledge.
Staiti, A. (2015). Praktische Identität aus phänomenologischer Sicht: Korsgaard und Husserl. *Phänomenol Forsch* 1: 171–188. https://doi.org/10.28937/1000107764
Tomasello, M. (2009). *Why we cooperate*. Cambridge: MIT Press.
Tomasello, M. (2016). *A natural history of human morality*. Cambridge and London: Harvard University Press.
Tomasello, M. (2019). *Becoming human: a theory of ontogeny*. Cambridge: Harvard University Press.
Verbeek, P.-P. (2008a). Cyborg intentionality: rethinking the phenomenology of human–technology relations. *Phenomenol Cogn Sci* 7: 387–395. https://doi.org/10.1007/s11097-008-9099-x
Verbeek, P.-P. (2008b). Obstetric ultrasound and the technological mediation of morality: a postphenomenological analysis. *Hum Stud* 31: 11–26. https://doi.org/10.1007/s10746-007-9079-0
Verbeek, P.-P. (2011). *Moralizing technology: understanding and designing the morality of things*. Chicago and London: University of Chicago Press.
Wallach, W., Allen, C. (2009). *Moral machines: teaching robots right from wrong*. Oxford: OUP.

Wedgwood, R. (2007). *The nature of normativity*. Oxford: OUP.
Wrangham, R. (2019). *The goodness paradox: the strange relationship between virtue and violence in human evolution*. New York: Pantheon.

Federico L.G. Faroldi

On the Human-Compatible Approach to the Alignment Problem: A Research Program

1. Introduction

As artificial agents become more intelligent, they might choose methods and means that are not aligned with humans' and that could have catastrophic consequences for humans and for the rest of the planet.

The general aim of this chapter is to discuss a solution the problem of AI alignment,[1] which has recently been proposed by computer scientist Stuart Russell and is the focus of intense research, the human-compatible approach. The human compatible approach suggests that intelligent agents be not required to maximize a simple given reward function attached to single goals, but to maximize the realization of human preferences, which are essentially uncertain.

This chapter will briefly describe the basic principles of the human compatible approach; it will then point out some problems that seem to have gone unnoticed in the literature; and it proposes some solutions to these problems.

These solutions, if and when fully carried out, aim to provide novel methods for norm- and value-based reasoning in AI systems, i.e., methods that will enable AI systems to comply not only with precise rules, but also with ethical principles and values, which are notoriously imprecise and hard to pin down. Thus this work is programmatic in scope, but will conclude with some methodological considerations.

This project contributes to the goal of preventing AI control by putting humans at the center of intelligent machine design, and does so uniquely by pooling expertise in philosophy, logic, and computer science.

---

1 See the next section for a brief discussion on the definition of alignment.

Section 2 introduces the Human-Compatible Approach, Section 3 introduces and discusses some open issues, Section 4 outlines some solutions that ideally contribute to the alignment problem.

2. The Human-Compatible Approach: the Basics

2.1 AGI, Alignment, Reinforcement Learning

This paper aims to contribute to a solution to the alignment problem.

Artificial general intelligence is the (hypothetical, for now) intelligence of a machine which can learn and reason to the full range of human abilities and potentially beyond. Many scientists believe that AGI will be reached within the end of the current century. (Some) Artificial intelligent agents are instructed to optimize a reward function, which is meant to represent effectively the combination of goals to be reached.[2] Even if it were possible to judge and weigh correctly all the subgoals, as agents become more intelligent (even without considering singularity scenarios), they might choose methods and means that are not aligned with humans' and that could have catastrophic consequences for humans and for the rest of the planet: this is the so-called AI alignment problem (cf e.g. Bostrom, 2014; Russell, 2019).[3]

The human compatible approach (Russell, 2019) suggests that intelligent agents be not required to maximize a simple given reward function attached to single goals, but to maximize the realization of human preferences, which are essentially uncertain. To reach this latter goal, current research is looking into inverse reinforcement learning (IRL), as originally studied in e.g. Ng and Russell, 2000.

---

[2] It is well-known, of course, that there might be a fairly large gap between the optimized reward function and the real reward function. This problem will be set aside in the present context, since it is not specific of the human-compatible approach and there is a lot of technical research devoted to it.

[3] How to properly define alignment is itself subject to intense debate. Gabriel (2020) identifies several definitions in the literature. For the purposes of this paper we can distinguish *intent* alignment, where an *A*gent is aligned with a *H*uman just in case A tries to do what H wants it to do; and *value or maximalist alignment,* where an Agent does what it ought to, as defined by an individual or society. The former definition is broadly inspired to Christiano's and Ngo's work (cf. e.g. Ngo 2020).

Contrary to reinforcement learning,[4] in IRL reward functions are not given, but have to be learnt: the agent observes the behavior of humans and has to learn their objectives, aims and values (i.e. infer their »reward function«), so that the AI, being uncertain about the »real« reward function, is expected to behave conservatively (e.g. to ask for confirmation before taking wild initiatives).

Before I put forward and discuss some problems with the human compatible framework, I introduce its main components and justifications.

2.2 The Human Compatible Approach

Russell proposes three principles to follow in order to create an aligned AI:

1. The machine's only objective is to maximize the realization of human preferences.
2. The machine is initially uncertain about what those preferences are.
3. The ultimate source of information about human preferences is human behaviour.

One can already ask whether humans do really have preferences in a real sense, or whether they are mere idealizations; and if so, how to aggregate the preferences of different humans in a consistent way. These problems are so deep that they have been discussed for decades; for the time being, however, for the argument's sake we assume that humans do have preferences and that there are ways to aggregate them consistently.

If the machine is uncertain about human preferences, Russell argues, it will be »humble«: it won't pursue single-mindedly one objective, and consequences be damned, but it will have to display epistemic humility, and allow itself to be switched off, if this is the human's preference.

The third principle has two functions: first, it provides a way for machines to know what the human preferences are, under the assumption that preferences and actions are related; the second aim is to make machines more useful as they go on and learn more about us.

4 Reinforcement learning is one of the basic machine learning approaches, where an agent acts in an environment in such a way as to maximize a cumulative reward.

Interestingly, Russell states: »there is no reason to suppose that machines who study our motivations will make the same choices, any more than criminologists become criminals (§ 7)«, but without argument.

A point to keep in mind is that Russell supposes that there is plenty of evidence of human preferences through their actions: direct evidence (observation) and indirect evidence (books, movies, the way we organized the world). Unfortunately, as a lot of research on action theory shows, it is not at all easy to say what is an action and what isn't. And while we humans have a pretty good ability to recognize most of the actions we encounter (although this is still difficult to do at acceptable standards, as criminal trials show), there is no reason to suppose that machine will be able to have the same ability, since they do not share the same kind of theory of mind we do.

There are of course some issues that Russell identifies and tackles: (i) learning preferences in the long run, as the machine acquires more and more information, it will become less and less uncertain about the human's preferences, thus being less deferent; (ii) missing some structures of preferences, such as those that are not expressed by a single value; (iii) the importance of motivation for and against actions, rather than just literal prohibition, due to the loophole principle; (iv) the pragmatic aspects of requests and instructions; (v) the problem of *wireheading*, where a machine hacks its own reward signal, due to a confusion between reward signals and actual rewards which should be avoided; (vi) recursive self-improvement; (vii) the fact that human are heterogeneous; (viii) the need for machines to make trade-offs among the preferences of different people.[5]

Russell assumes a broadly consequentialist framework, for he thinks that we build machines to bring about consequences, and in the absence of self-awareness it is futile to build machines that are virtuous or deontological. Consequentialism has its share of philosophical problems, but in this context two stand out: interpersonal comparisons of utilities and comparisons across different population sizes, coupled with making decisions under moral uncertainty.

When it comes to mistakes, here's an illuminating quote:

> when Lee Sedol lost his Go match to AlphaGo, he played one or more moves that guaranteed he would lose, and AlphaGo could (in some

5 I can't possibly comment on all these issues in this context; Russell himself discusses some solution in Ch. 7.

> cases at least) detect that he had done this. It would be incorrect, however, for AlphaGo to infer that Lee Sedol has a preference for losing. Instead, it would be reasonable to infer that Lee Sedol has a preference for winning but has some computational limitations that prevent him from choosing the right move in all cases. Thus, in order to understand Lee Sedol's behavior and learn about his preferences, a robot following the third principle (»the ultimate source of information about human preferences is human behavior«) has to understand something about the cognitive processes that generate his behavior. It cannot assume he is rational. […] it makes sense from a practical point of view to look at the major ways in which humans deviate from rationality and to study how to learn preferences from behavior that exhibits such deviations (Russell 2019, § 9).

It is very important, thus, that machines understand motivations. Motivations sometimes can be reduced to preferences, but it seems that there are some motivations that are not preferences. I argue elsewhere that the right theoretical concept here is that of a reason. Some reasons are motivational, and explain why people are motivated to do certain things.[6]

There are at least three kinds of uncertainty about preference: epistemic, computational, and ordinary: for the first, you don't know what your preference is, but you can find out empirically; for the second, you need more computational resources; for the third, you need to resolve the uncertainty about the world, e.g. about the future.

Another issue is preference change.[7] This change is present both at a personal level, and at a societal level. Preference change differs from preference update, which is the process of adjourning preferences when new evidence is available. Preference change instead does not depend on new evidence. Preference change is problematic for two reasons: the first is that it is not clear which preferences should count: those at the time of the decision, or those at the time of the effects; the second is that, contrary to preference update, preference change seems to be brute, i.e. not subject to rational constraints.

Preference change elicits an issue for machines, e.g. the fact that machines can try to change human preferences: »Why might an intelligent machine deliberately set out to modify the preferences of

[6] F. Faroldi, Reasons-based AI Ethics, ms 2023.

[7] There is a fairly large literature on preference change. I refer the reader to the excellent Pettigrew 2019. This issue will be discussed again in Sect. 4 in the context of my outlined solution.

humans? The answer is quite simple: to make the preferences easier to satisfy (ib).«

I have introduced the basic components of Russell's Human-Compatible approach and I have reported some of the basic issues he himself raises. In the next section, I will introduce and discuss some novel problems for the Human-Compatible approach.

3. Problems with the human compatible framework.

In this section I raise some novel problems for the human-compatible approach, especially from a philosophical perspective. I discuss three orders of problems with this framework. Some will get a more detailed treatment than others.

> **Problem 1**: if you are a IRL agent, all you can ever observe is behavior, but (i) it is hard to analyze it into the underlying *beliefs and values*, which are directly unobservable and (ii) there is also unobserved behavior (i.e. very rare or impossible), crucial for *counterfactual or counterpossible reasoning* (i.e. counterfactuals with (necessarily) false antecedents), which is relevant both to reach higher intelligence (cf. Pearl, 2000) and to ascribe responsibility; however, one of the most popular tool to handle counterfactual reasoning in AI (the causal Bayesian networks of Pearl, 2000) is based on intensional logics, which cannot handle non-omniscient agents and cannot entertain counterpossible scenarios;
>
> **Problem 2**: (iii) modeling often relies on behavior that is assumed to be *optimal* (coherent, full knowledge, etc.), or agents that are idealized, while it should be able to understand when humans make mistakes; (iv) at any given time, there are many reward functions for which an observed behavior is optimal (*degeneracy*);
>
> **Problem 3**: (v) even if the preceding strategy is successful, at a certain point the AI will have learnt all there is to learn, and therefore behave as a *utility maximizer*, thus recreating all the problems of misalignment, because current approaches to normative uncertainty (cf. MacAskill et al, 2020) assign a probability distribution to value theories (utilities), thus assum-

ing that there is one true utility function. In other terms, the uncertainty is epistemic, not ontological, and is stationary (i.e. agents' preference do not change over time).

4. An Outline for some Solutions

4.1 Some Research Objectives in a Programmatic Spirit.

The general aim of the approach sketched here is to contribute to a human compatible solution the problem of AI alignment as limited to some of the issues (i)–(v) above. The final aim is to provide novel methods for norm- and value-based reasoning in AI systems, i.e., methods that will enable AI systems to comply not only with precise rules, but also with ethical principles and values. This results in (super)intelligent machines being dependent on humans at a deep level (due to the constant learning needed to reconstruct our values), rather than *viceversa,* and in integrating (super)intelligent agents in our *Wertanschauung*. The general approach I suggest to adopt is based on further refining the Human Compatible approach in the direction of fine-grained logics and value indeterminacy.

The approach has the following more precise objectives to solve the aforementioned Problems 1–3:

Objective 1: Integrate realistic/fine-grained counterfactual reasoning into inverse reinforcement learning, thus addressing Problem 1 (issues (i)–(ii)) and Problem 2, issue (iii).

Objective 2: Develop an account where human values are essentially (ontologically) imprecise, thus addressing Problem 2 issue (iv) and Problem 3 (issue (v)).

Objective 3: Validate and test the developed framework, implementing corrections when needed.

The expected result is both a formal and a substantial contribution to the current effort to reach artificial general intelligence which integrates computer science and philosophical expertise.

In a programmatic spirit, let me note down some more concrete steps to reach the objectives:

> **W.r.t. Objective 1**: specify a hyperintensional semantics for counterfactual reasoning.[8] First, such an approach would be able to discriminate between logical and necessary equivalents, and it is therefore finer-grained than intensional approaches. Such a feature is necessary both if intelligent artificial agents have to understand humans' preferences, given that humans have cognitive limitations precluding logical omniscience, and to avoid the optimality problem.

In order to develop a fine-grained approach to counterfactual reasoning, the framework of choice is truthmaker semantics, which has been proposed by Kit Fine (cf. Fine, 2017), and which I further refined to be applied to deontic reasoning, the logic of responsibility, and reasons (cf. Faroldi, 2019).

> **W.r.t. Objective 2**: Develop a formal approach to uncertain values using imprecise value functions. Once we know which states there are, which are merely possible, and which are impossible and how to counterfactually reason with them, we need to be able to infer reward functions. We need to know how agents value states. Given the set of states Ω, a suitably generated structure F of its subsets, we define M as a (finite) family of partial indexed signed measures μ_i^α, $i \in I$, $s.\ t.\ \mu_i^\alpha\ \boldsymbol{F} \rightarrow R$, which generate an interval of values, rather than a single value, for each agent α ∈ A.[9]

> **W.r.t. Objective 3**: Validate and test the developed framework with benchmark cases (such as the trolley problem). Apply the fine-grained framework so that agents can estimate their own responsibility and study the consequences of this proposal at the normative and application level, by introducing a notion of legal personality for artificial agents and attenuating the notion of strict (or product) liability for the creators. Two necessary elements of responsibility ascriptions, according to the mainstream

8 A context is hyperintensional if it does not admit substitution of logical or intensional equivalents *salva veritate*.

9 A close relative of this account was developed to deal with value disagreement in Faroldi, 2021.

stances (Talbert, 2019) are the possibility of doing otherwise and the value or disvalue of a course of conduct. These elements open the possibility for AGI to participate in humans legal and moral practices of responsibility attribution.

Case 1: Paperclip Scenario

Consider the paperclip scenario, where an AGI is tasked with maximizing paperclip production. Unaligned scenarios where the AGI destroys the rest of the universe to produce paperclip, prevents a switch-off, engages in wireheading, resists changes to the reward function are already »solved« by the human compatible approach: by maximizing human preferences, which are uncertain, all these problems would be avoided. However, human preferences and values are learnt by observation of human's behavior. But there's no behavior to observe when it comes to very important but catastrophic events, that never realized before: the destruction of the human race, or the provoked extinction of entire species. As applied to the paperclip problem, the current project steps in to provide tools to (i) take into account reasoning with unobserved situations via counterfactual reasoning (what would happen if all iron in the universe would be consumed to produce paperclips? would it still make sense to maximize paperclip production if no humans lived anymore?), in (ii) a highly fine-grained (hyperintensional) way, by taking into account a range of values, rather than one, to take into account the problem of assigning values to unobserved states (the extinction of a random species vs the extinction of an iron-eating bacterium if iron is depleted vs the extinction of a parasite species), to the fact that there are very different humans who might disagree, normative uncertainty, etc.

Case 2: Self-driving cars and the trolley problem

A famous benchmark case in moral philosophy is the trolley problem. There's a trolley about to hit *n* people, but by pressing a switch the trolley modifies its direction and only 1 person is hit. Different moral theories have different positions on what to do.

How should an AGI behave? And how will it? In a traditional IRL setting, when confronted with a trolley problem, an autonomous vehicle should observe the behavior of experts and extract their reward function.

In the proposal developed in the current project, an autonomous vehicle would have to consider counterpossible scenarios, in order to take into account their value. While this cannot be obviously observed, it is a highly relevant point that is used to compare different version of utilitarianism. Moreover, it will only consider value intervals, rather than single outputs, to off-set the chance that different moral theories might be right, or that an average of moral theories is taken while they are incomparable.

4.2. Methodological Remarks

The present research program intends to blend research in logic and computer science with research in informal areas of ethics and philosophy. This mix has the particular aim, on one hand, to dispense with simplifying assumptions that are quite widespread in technical fields (omniscience, that all behavior is observable, that there exists one true value function) by taking on board the complexity of humans' normative life and, on the other hand, to try and make more precise (and usable) some of theories and concepts of more humanistic disciplines (normative uncertainty, responsibility).

Instead of the traditional intensional approach based on possible worlds, which are consistent, complete, and flat, truthmakers are states that are not necessarily assumed to be consistent, complete and that are equipped with a mereological structure. This set-up is more adequate for agents with limited capabilities having to reason with real-world information, which is possibly incomplete and contradictory, but can be expanded. Moreover, this framework has been shown to be able to handle well non-causal explanations (cf. e.g. grounding), which makes it an ideal choice not just for counterfactuals, but also for counterpossibles. The framework developed by Fine, 2012 should be integrated with the Bayesian networks approach developed in e.g. Pearl, 2000 to reach Objective 1, rather than with standard intensional semantics.

This project assumes that human values are essentially imprecise. This can capture the sort of value uncertainty that is thought to be necessary for alignment within the human compatible framework. In contrast to some of the current approaches to normative uncertainty (cf. MacAskill et al, 2020), which assign a probability distribution to value theories (utilities), here each value function is imprecise, i.e. does not result in sharp values but in an interval of values.

Imprecise values, coupled with the ability to reason about what could have been, make it possible to know what should have been and what could and should be, all essential elements in the ascription of responsibility. Ascribing (and self-ascribing) responsibility to intelligent agents is one way to integrate in an ethical way humans and general intelligent agents, for it avoids the problem of an agent turning into an utility maximizer: there is always the possibility of being responsible looming ahead.

The main conceptual limitation of the testing phase is that the framework, when fully developed, is about AGI, which we don't have yet. The testing will then have to be on smaller available components.

5 Conclusion and Further Work

This chapter is both introductory and programmatic in spirit: first, it aimed at introducing the fundamentals of the Human Compatible Approach developed by Stuart Russell to a philosophically-minded audience; second, it discussed some known problems and some open issues of the account; third and finally, it proposed an outline of a research program geared towards solving some of these issues by means of a stronger integration into contemporary philosophical and logical research.[10]

References

Awad, Edmond, Sohan Dsouza, Azim Shariff, Iyad Rahwan, and Jean-François Bonnefon. 2020. Universals and variations in moral decisions made in 42 countries by 70,000 participants. *Proceedings of the National Academy of Sciences*, 117, 5, pp. 2332–2337.

Bostrom, Nick. 2014. *Superintelligence: paths, dangers, strategies*, Oxford: Oxford University Press.

[10] Many thanks for interesting discussions and objections to Stuart Russell, members of the Center for Human-Compatible AI at UC Berkeley, Julie Mennes, and my students in Pavia.

Faroldi, Federico L. G. 2019. *Hyperintensionality and Normativity*. Dordrecht: Springer.

Faroldi, Federico L. G. 2021. Towards a Logic of Value and Disagreement via Imprecise Measures. *Bulletin of the Section of Logic*, 50, 2, pp. 131–149.

Faroldi, Federico L. G. *Reasons-based AI Ethics*, ms., 2023.

Fine, Kit. 2012. Counterfactuals without Possible Worlds. *Journal of Philosophy*, 109, 3, pp. 221–246.

Fine, Kit. 2017. Truthmaker Semantics. In: *A Companion to the Philosophy of Language*, ed. by Bob Hale, Crispin Wright, and Alexander Miller, 2nd ed., ms, Blackwell, London, pp. 556–77.

Gabriel, Iason. 2020. Artificial Intelligence, Values, and Alignment. *Minds and Machine*.

Ng, A. Y. and Stuart Russell. 2000. Algorithms for inverse reinforcement learning. In: *Proc. 17th Intl. Conf. on Machine Learning* (ICML-2000), ed. by P. Langley, Morgan Kaufmann, pp. 663–670.

Ngo, Richard. 2020 *AI Safety from First Principles*, ms.

Pearl, Judea. 2000. *Causality: Models, Reasoning, and Inference*. Cambridge: Cambridge University Press.

Pettigrew, Richard. 2019. *Choosing for Changing Selves*. Oxford: Oxford University Press.

Russell, Stuart. 2019. *Human Compatible: Artificial Intelligence and the Problem of Control*. Viking.

Talbert, Matthew. 2019. Moral Responsibility. In: *The Stanford Encyclopedia of Philosophy*, ed. by Edward N. Zalta, Winter 2019, Metaphysics Research Lab, Stanford University.

MacAskill, William, Krister Bykvist and Toby Ord. 2020. *Moral Uncertainty*. Oxford: Oxford University Press.

Abstracts

The transition from might to right: male-male conflict and the evolution of **Homo duplex***

Richard Wrangham

In *Civilization and its Discontents*, Sigmund Freud (1989: 49) claimed that »Human life in common is only made possible when a majority comes together which is stronger than any separate individual and which remains united against all separate individuals… The power of this community is then set up as ›right‹ in opposition to the power of the individual, which is condemned as ›brute force‹.« By suggesting that the concept of ›right‹ emerged out of primitive power dynamics Freud produced an idea that underlies a contemporary theory of the origin of much morality. In this chapter I show that Freud's speculation is well supported, because humans are the only primates in which societies are dominated not by independent tyrants but by coalitions that have ultimate power. A crucial question for understanding human communal action, therefore, is why groups dominated by unconstrained tyrants gave way to societies led by communal action. I consider two major kinds of explanation. The execution hypothesis proposes that adult males cooperated in executing tyrants using pre-conceived plans or understandings. The alliances that adult males used to kill tyrants then became social weapons used to impose group norms for the benefit of those males. The execution hypothesis is supported by much ethnographic, genetic, fossil and comparative evidence. The intergroup aggression hypothesis, which is the most popular alternative explanation, proposes that intense warfare could have favoured cooperation among adult males at the expense of tyrants. This idea faces a series of difficulties, including the puzzle of why it should apply only to humans. I conclude that the transition from might to right occurred as a result of humans became skilled at using alliances to cheaply kill tyrants. The result is *Homo duplex*, a species governed by the conflicting motivations of selfishness and groupishness.

Norms, Rights, Obligations: An Attempt at Empirical Reduction

Edoardo Fittipaldi

Among the manners empirical scientists use »norm«, »right«, and »obligation«, are *normative explanations*, that is, hypotheses stating that some individual's behavior is *caused* by their following a norm according to which, say, they *should*, *can*, or *have the right/obligation* to act that way. What are these theoretical entities, which sometimes are used even to explain *non-human* behaviors? How can we distinguish between normative and economic behavior? In this chapter, Fittipaldi offers a stipulative definition for »norm« whose aim is to offer a criterion for distinguishing between normative and economic behavior (1) without having recourse to obscure terms like »should«, »obligation«, »can«, »right«, (2) and by reducing these latter to empirical phenomena. Norms are conceptualized as psychical dispositions to experience normative emotions toward certain behaviors. This definition is not circular as *normative* emotions are defined in a non-normative way, that is, as the innate and »learned« emotions that, respectively, get reshaped or emerge during the child's primary socialization *provided that* (α) this process is conditioned by the fact that the child conceives of her caregiver in the manner monotheisms conceive of the One God and (β) this conception unconsciously influences the way those emotions are experienced during adolescence and adulthood. Based on this definition, Fittipaldi (i) discusses different types of norms depending on the emotion that back them, (ii) reconceptualizes the notions of *right* and *obligation*, and (iii) argues that in certain connections it may make sense to speak of the existence of proto-norms, proto-rights, para-guilt, etc., and so even when discussing non-human animal behavior.

The Normativity of Norms

John J. Drummond

This chapter is rooted in two distinctions: (1) first-order norms versus second-order norms and (2) first-order normativity versus second-order normativity. First-order norms are embedded in our understanding of what it takes to be successful in an undertaking, and these norms are adjusted in the reflective adjustment and advancement of that understanding. The normativity of these norms arises in our commitment to take these norms (or a reflective modification thereof) as binding on our thoughts, attitudes, and actions. Second-order norms, by contrast, are rooted in the nature of rational agency as such. It is by virtue of the essential structures of rational agency that we can achieve truthfulness in the first-order norms. There is a kind of necessity attaching to second-order norms, although it is not a practical necessity. An agent can fail as an agent by not adhering to these norms. Moreover, it is by appeal to the second-order norms and their normativity that the critique of first-order norms, both within and across cultures, is possible.

The Ethnologist's Judgment: Maurice Merleau-Ponty and Raymond Aron on Interpreting Culture

Alessio Rotundo

The critique of cultural relativism does not involve the dismissal of pluralism itself, which can be rehabilitated from the point of view of a hierarchy of cultural patterns. The affirmation of a hierarchy of culture patterns does not necessarily imply dogmatic ideas about cultural values, contempt of other cultures, and barbarism. In this paper, I discuss the positions of Maurice Merleau-Ponty and Raymon Aron. Despite the diversity of their approaches, in their moral diagnosis of modernity, both Merleau-Ponty and Aron converge around a critique of the relativistic viewpoint put forward by the anthropology of Claude Lévi-Strauss. Aron points out the epistemological and moral ambiguity of the egalitarian viewpoint in anthropology, which is based on the idea that every human pattern is original and every human expression is essential. If this were really so, then every culture could only be evaluated with respect to itself, which would imply the impossibility of comparing cultures with each other as well as of opposing barbarism. For Merleau-Ponty, the absolutism of plurality is contradictory because it does not recognize the cultural and historical standpoint of its own viewpoint, that is, the viewpoint of the culture raising the question about its own relationship with other cultures and about the possibility of a pluralist human society. Aron's proposal of a »pluralist anthropology« and Merleau-Ponty's theory of »historical symbolism« converge around the idea of an ethics predicated on plurality that is not incompatible with a reflection on the meaning of rational humanity in history.

Aftificial Intelligence and Quasi-Normativity: Some Indications for a Solution to the Normative Question in the Field of AI Ethics

Roberto Redaelli

This chapter aims to investigate the notion of digital normativity, understood as the binding force exerted on the human subject by the predictions and standards established by artificial intelligent systems. To this end, we focus our attention on the merits and limits of the recent treatment of digital normativity proposed by Fourneret and Yvert, in order to bring a decisive correction to their ideas through the introduction of the notion of quasi-normativity. In order to introduce and develop this notion in the context of enquiry into the digital sphere, we make use of Don Ihde's precise postphenomenological considerations on the nature of the artificial agent as a quasi-other. With the aid of Ihde's postphenomenological approach and the introduction of the notion of quasi-normativity, we intend to shed new light on the binding force of AI and offer some guidance for the resolution of the normative question in intelligent systems.

On the Human-Compatible Approach to the Alignment Problem: A Research Program

Federico L.G. Faroldi

This chapter aims to contribute to the issue of artificial general intelligence (AGI) alignment in a programmatic spirit, by suggesting some improvements on the human-compatible approach of Russell 2019.

List of Contributors

John J. Drummond is the Robert Southwell, S.J. Distinguished Professor Emeritus of Philosophy and the Humanities at Fordham University. He is the author of *Husserlian Intentionality and Non-Foundational Realism* (Kluwer) and *A Historical Dictionary of Husserl's Philosophy* (2nd ed., Rowman & Littlefield). He has edited or co-edited seven collections of articles on phenomenology, including the recently published *Emotional Experiences: Ethical and Social Significance* (Rowman & Littlefield International), and has written extensively on intentionality, the emotions, and ethics.

Federico L.G. Faroldi is associate professor of philosophy, law and artificial intelligence at the University of Pavia, Italy, and director of the Normative Risk Lab. He was previously Senior Researcher in Bern (Switzerland), where he directed an Ambizione project (SNSF), Senior Researcher of the Flanders Research Foundation (FWO) at Ghent University (Belgium) and Lise Meitner Fellow of the Austrian Science Fund (FWF) in Austria. He has studied or worked in Pisa, Florence, St Andrews, Oxford, ENS Rue d'Ulm (Paris), New York University, University of Southern California and the Center for Human-Compatible AI at UC Berkeley. His main interests are deontic logic, hyperintensionality, formal ethics, and the philosophy of AI. His most recent book is *Hyperintensionality and Normativity* (Springer).

Edoardo Fittipaldi is a full professor of Sociology of Law at the State University of Milan, where he graduated in law in 1999. During his PhD, he studied Critical Rationalism under the supervision of the German philosopher and sociologist Hans Albert. Next, he studied in Poland both Petrażycki's psychological theory of normative phenomena and its main developments. His research focuses (1) on the re-foundation of Petrażycki's theory of normativity on psychoanalysis and contemporary psychology, (2) on its cross-fertilization with classical legal sociology (especially that of Max Weber and Theodor Geiger), and (3) on the development of a Petrażyckian legal dogmatics—that is, a legal dogmatics at the service of the Principle of Legality—by making use of forms of non-standard logic. He published several essays and articles in English, Italian, and Russian. In English, he published *Everyday Legal Ontology: A Psychological and Linguistic Investigation within the Framework of Leon Petrażycki's Theory of Law* (2012, LED), and edited *Revisiting John Searle on Deriving »Ought« from »Is«* (2021, with Paolo Di Lucia, Palgrave Macmillan) and *Leon Petrażycki: Law, Emotions, Society* (2023, with A. Javier Treviño, Routledge).

Roberto Redaelli is currently postdoctoral researcher in Philosophy at the University of Milan and Lecturer at the University of Nürnberg-Erlangen. He also serves as adjunct Professor at the Department of Mathematics of the University of Pavia, where he teaches Ethics of Artificial Intelligence. He received his PhD from the University of Milan. He has been a visiting scholar at the University of Heidelberg and at the Husserl Archive of Freiburg im Breisgau. He is author of several publications concerning neo-Kantian philosophy, philosophical anthropology, phenomenology, and post-phenomenology.

Alessio Rotundo obtained his doctorate in philosophy from Duquesne University, Pittsburgh in 2020. He studied philosophy at the University of Turin in Italy, the University of Heidelberg in Germany, the University of Kentucky under the *Baden-Württemberg Stipendium,* and at the École Normale Supérieure in Paris supported by the *Bourse Chateaubriand.* His research interests and publications focus on topics in twentieth-century Continental philosophy and the history of modern and contemporary philosophy, especially in the fields of phenomenology and philosophical hermeneutics. He is author of *First Nature: The Problem of Nature in the Phenomenology of Merleau-Ponty,* published by Brill (2023). This book explores a radically integrative phenomenology of nature across foundational aspects of human experience: sense perception, organic development and behavior, cognition, language, and history. He currently serves as Adjunct Professor at Xavier University of Louisiana and Loyola University New Orleans.

Richard Wrangham is the Moore Research Professor of Biological Anthropology in the Department of Human Evolutionary Biology at Harvard University, Boston, MA, USA. He studied chimpanzee behavior in Tanzania for his 1975 PhD at Cambridge University (UK). In 1987 he founded the Kibale Chimpanzee Project in Uganda, which has documented the behavioral biology of a community of wild chimpanzees ever since. His books include *Demonic Males: Apes and the Origins of Human Violence* (Houghton Mifflin, 1996, with Dale Peterson), *Catching Fire: How Cooking Made Us Human* (Basic Books, 2009) and *The Goodness Paradox: The Strange Relationship Between Virtue and Violence in Human Evolution* (Pantheon, January 2019).

Kolibri 360 GmbH
Ferdinand-Jühlke-Straße 7
99095 Erfurt, Deutschland
produktsicherheit@kolibri360.de